Context 21

VOCABi

Cornelsen

AF196149

Abbreviations and symbols used in VOCABI

abbr.	abbreviation	**p.**	page	
A	adjective	**pl**	plural	
ADV	adverb	PRON	pronoun	
AE	American English	**sb.**	somebody	
BE	British English	**sing**	singular	
ca.	circa (= about)	**sth.**	something	
cf.	confer, see	**usu.**	usually	
e.g.	(Latin) exempli gratia = for example	V	verb	
esp.	especially			
etc.	(Latin) et cetera = and so on	◀▶	antonym/opposite	
etw.	etwas	!	Careful! Mistakes are often made here.	
fml	formal	☆	American pronunciation follows. (As a rule, regular differences in AE pronunciation like the [r] after vowels are not given.)	
i.e.	(Latin) id est = that is, in other words			
infml	informal			
jd.	jemand			
jdm.	jemandem			
jdn.	jemanden			
N	noun			

VOCAB Notes

These notes will help you with the language in the texts. A full list is on pages 6–7.

GET THE CONTEXT

Here you can find further information, facts and illustrations to help you understand the context of the themes.

CHECKPOINT In English, please!

The optional CHECKPOINTS encourage you to test your understanding of relevant phrases in the texts. Suggested answers are supplied on pages 172–177.

Blue highlighting

marks the words and phrases which you should learn or revise.

Blue underlining

refers to an entry in the 'VOCAB Notes' or 'GET THE CONTEXT'.

Welcome to VOCABI – your essential tool
for learning and revising VOCAB in the 'Oberstufe'!

With **VOCABI** you can practise, expand and improve your knowledge of relevant words and phrases from 15 essential topics in 'Oberstufe' English and the 'Abitur'. It can be used with any textbook or collection of texts.

Read and learn the 'Words in Context' from the *Context 21* Student's Book, with added explanations, English-German word lists and notes on collocations, word families and usage.

The unique combination of texts and language support makes **VOCABI** a handy, versatile learning aid for use at school, at home or literally anywhere.

VOCABI – compact word power at your fingertips

- ► **Study** the tips at the beginning of the book and develop your VOCAB Skills.
- ► **See** the words you need to learn in clear, interesting contexts.
- ► **Support** your learning with hints on usage, related words, pronunciation and common mistakes.
- ► **Sharpen** your knowledge of thematic VOCAB for class tests or 'Klausuren'.
- ► **Stimulate** your interest in important topics for essays and discussions.
- ► **Search** for individual words in the VOCAB Finder at the back of the book.

Contents

List of VOCAB Notes

VOCAB Skills

1   Dealing with unknown words

Here are some 'guessing techniques' you can use to work out the meaning of new words you read or hear:

- Look at the context of the new word. Headings, subtitles, pictures and charts can help you.
- Work out the word class of the new word (e.g. noun, verb or adjective). This will help you to get closer to what you are looking for.
- Think of words from the same word family that you may know:
  - **muscular** ['mʌskjələ] from **muscle** ['mʌsl],
  - **denial** from **deny**.
- Look out for suffixes and prefixes:
  - **environment*alist*:**
    environment + *-al* = 'referring to the environment',
    environmental + *-ist* = 'a person who is concerned with protecting the environment',
  - **un*predict*able*:**
    predict ('foresee') + *-able* = 'able to be foreseen',
    un- + **predictable** = 'unable to be foreseen',
  - *in*famous** ['ɪnfəməs]:
    in- + **famous** ('well known') = 'well known, but for negative reasons'.

- Think of words you might know from another language:
  - **proposition** from the French **proposer** ('suggest'),
  - **embellish** ('make sth. more beautiful') from the French **belle** ('beauty'),
  - **commercial** (German *kommerziell*).

  However, beware of false friends:
  - **sensible** ≠ German *sensibel*,
  - **chef** [ʃef] ≠ German *Chef/in*.
- When listening or watching, you need to work fast. So pay attention to the following as well:
  - the general topic of conversation,
  - facial expressions, gestures and tone of voice,
  - the reactions of others involved in the conversation.

> ### TIP
> Remember that you do not need to understand every word you read or hear. You only need to start dealing with unknown words when you think they are essential for understanding the text or the conversation.

2 Paraphrasing

Paraphrasing is useful when you don't know an English word or phrase that you need or want to use, e.g. in a conversation or when mediating. It allows you to get across the meaning without using the word or phrase itself.

Here are some paraphrasing techniques:

- You can use synonyms or antonyms:
  - It's the same as 'freedom'.
    (► **liberty**)
  - It's the opposite of 'increase'.
    (► **decrease**)
- You can use a word of general meaning (e.g. **somebody**) or a word that expresses what kind of thing you mean (e.g. **a tool**). Then you add a phrase or clause (often a relative clause) with more details, e.g. what the thing does, what it can be used for or where you can find it.
  - Do you mean somebody who offers to work and help people, but doesn't ask for any money in return?
    (► **a volunteer**)
  - It's a tool for making holes in a sheet of paper.
    (► **a hole punch**)

'Woof, woof, woof – but I'm paraphrasing.'

- Paraphrases sometimes include adjectives:
  It's a <u>big</u> shop that sells all kinds of things.
  (► **a department store**)
- It may help to add an extra sentence to show what you mean:
  It's a kind of hard hat that you wear to protect your head. <u>Motorcyclists and American footballers wear them.</u>
  (► **a crash helmet**)
- In some cases a fuller explanation is needed:
  It's a saying and means you should help and care for your own family, etc. before you start helping other people.
  (► **Charity begins at home.**)
- The definitions used in monolingual dictionaries (cf. p.11) are similar to paraphrases.

3 Learning new words

Here are some hints for learning new words. Find out which method is best for you.

- Learn synonyms (e.g. **terrible, awful, horrible**) and/or antonyms (e.g. **agree ◊ disagree**) together.
- There are many words in English that are derived from or made up of other words. VOCABI will help you to learn word families (e.g. **emigrate, emigrant, emigration**) instead of just individual words.
- Group words and phrases into word fields according to topic (e.g. **money matters: cash, bank account, interest rate**). You can make lists or arrange the words in networks. Include words you already know.
- Context is very important. Knowing how to use a word instantly makes it more memorable. Learn how words go together in collocations (e.g. **a big problem, a large family, a great success**).
- Make bilingual flash cards to test yourself. This can be a good way to pass the time while on the bus to school, etc.
- Write new words on Post-it notes and stick them around your bedroom so you will see them repeatedly.

Front of flash card   Back of flash card

- Make the most of modern technology and load vocabulary software onto your smartphone, MP3 player, etc.
- Set aside 10 minutes a day for memorizing vocabulary. But don't try to learn more than 7–10 words at a time. Also, choose your time carefully. Many scientists claim that a human brain is more capable of absorbing information just before sleep.

TIP
Make an effort to use your new vocabulary as soon as possible. It then passes from passive vocabulary into active use and you won't forget it.

4 Using a dictionary

A dictionary is much more than just a tool for finding out the meaning of words. A monolingual dictionary, for example, is perfect if you are looking for examples of typical usages and synonyms.

To get the most out of your dictionary, you should familiarize yourself with its layout. Make sure you know the abbreviations and symbols used and study the complete entries. Here is an example from the *Oxford Advanced Learner's Dictionary*:

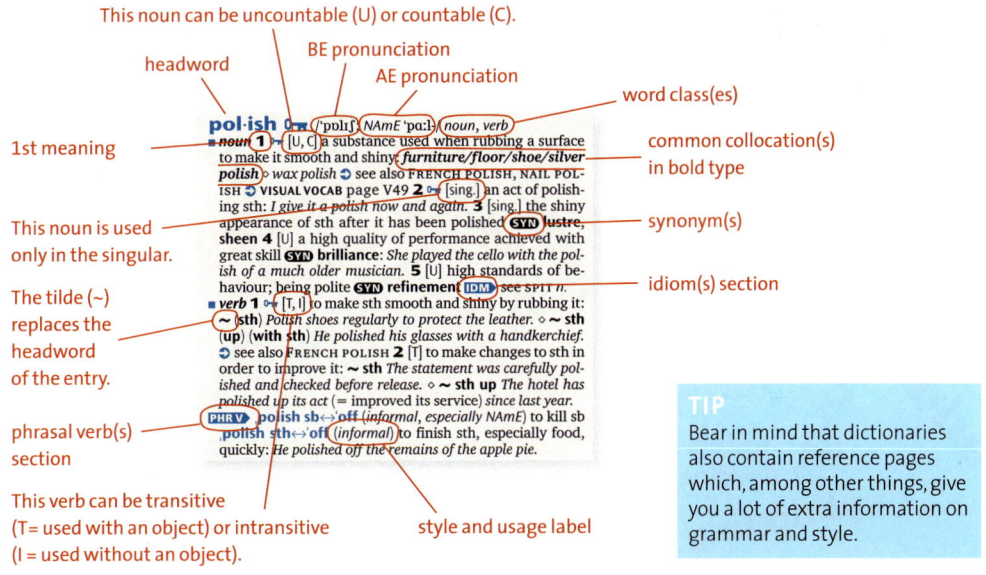

This noun can be uncountable (U) or countable (C).

BE pronunciation

AE pronunciation

headword

word class(es)

1st meaning

common collocation(s) in bold type

This noun is used only in the singular.

synonym(s)

The tilde (~) replaces the headword of the entry.

idiom(s) section

phrasal verb(s) section

This verb can be transitive (T= used with an object) or intransitive (I = used without an object).

style and usage label

TIP

Bear in mind that dictionaries also contain reference pages which, among other things, give you a lot of extra information on grammar and style.

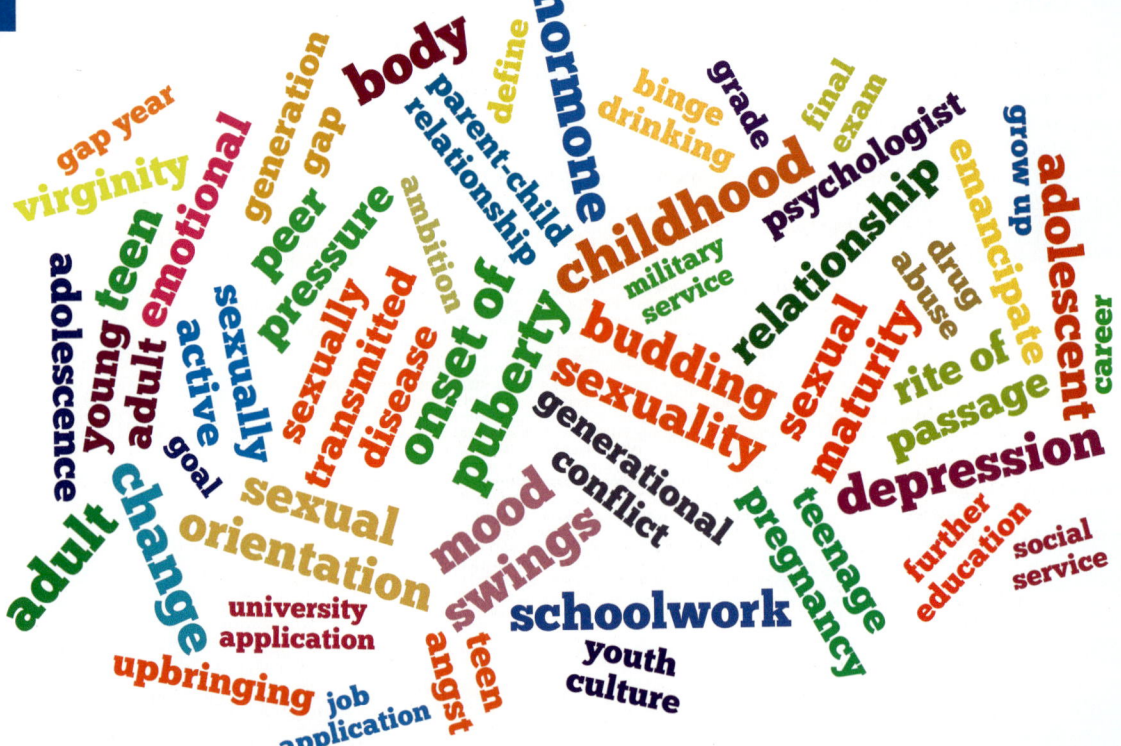

Being Young

1   From childhood to adolescence

2   Sex and sexuality

3   Teenage emancipation

4   Planning your future

1 From childhood to adolescence

Childhood is supposed to be a <u>carefree</u> time during which one is protected by one's parents and other responsible adults.

Then, with the onset of puberty, life suddenly becomes com-
5 plicated. One's body changes, and hormones often cause mood swings that may take teens from great happiness to deep depression in no time. Adolescents suddenly want to sleep in and stay up late. It becomes harder for them to concentrate on schoolwork as they discover other interests, not the least of
10 which is girls or boys – depending on their <u>sexual orientation</u>.

'Don't call me a teenager. From now on, I want to be referred to as a pre-adult.'

'carefree' – 'careless'

carefree *sorgenfrei, unbekümmert*
careless *nachlässig, unvorsichtig*

Collocations with 'orientation'

<u>sexual orientation</u> [ˌsekʃuəlˌɔːriənˈteɪʃn]
sexuelle Orientierung (d.h., ob jemand heterosexuell oder homosexuell ist)
religious orientation [rɪˈlɪdʒəs] *religiöse Überzeugung, Glaubensrichtung*
political orientation [pəˈlɪtɪkl] *politische Einstellung / Überzeugung*

CHECKPOINT — *In English, please!*

a *Das Leben wird plötzlich kompliziert.*
b *ausschlafen*
c *lange aufbleiben*
d *sich auf die Schule konzentrieren*

1 **childhood** [ˈtʃaɪldhʊd]	*Kindheit*	**have a happy / an unhappy / a tough childhood** *eine glückliche / eine unglückliche / eine schwere Kindheit haben* **from/since childhood** *von Kindheit an*
3 **adult** [ˈædʌlt, əˈdʌlt]	*Erwachsene(r)*	= **grown-up** (meist Kindersprache) N **adulthood** *Erwachsenenalter, Erwachsensein*
4 **the onset of puberty** [ˈɒnset, ˈpjuːbəti]	*das Einsetzen der Pubertät, der Beginn der Pubertät*	! stress: <u>**puberty**</u> [ˈ---] No article: **reach/hit** (infml)**/enter puberty** *in die Pubertät kommen* **go through puberty** *in der Pubertät sein/stecken, pubertieren*
5 **one's body changes**	*der eigene Körper verändert sich*	**change 1.** *etw. (ver)ändern;* **2.** *sich (ver)ändern*
hormone [ˈhɔːməʊn]	*Hormon*	! stress: <u>**hormone**</u> [ˈ--] A **hormonal** [hɔːˈməʊnl]
mood swings (usu. pl)	*Stimmungsschwankungen*	**be in a good/bad mood** *gute/schlechte Laune haben, gut/schlecht drauf sein*
6 **teen** (infml, esp. AE)	*Teenager, Teen*	= **teenager** A **teen** *jugendlich, Teenager...*
7 **depression** [dɪˈpreʃn]	*Depression, Niedergeschlagen- heit*	A **depressed** [dɪˈprest] *deprimiert; nieder- geschlagen*
adolescent [ˌædəˈlesnt]	*Jugendliche(r), Heranwachsende(r)*	A **adolescent** *heranwachsend, jugendlich* N **adolescence** [ˌædəˈlesns] *Jugend, Pubertät*
9 **schoolwork**	*Arbeit in der Schule, Arbeit für die Schule*	cf. **homework** *Hausaufgaben*

2 Sex and sexuality

A teenager's budding sexuality is not without problems. Although their bodies have reached sexual maturity, some teenagers may not be ready to handle the emotional side of a relationship. Quite often they experience peer pressure to become sexually active, even though they may not yet want to.

On the other hand, quite a few young adults see losing their virginity as just another rite of passage and have sex without regard for the consequences, which explains the high rates of teenage pregnancy and sexually transmitted diseases.

15

Word family 'sex'

N **sex** 1. *Geschlecht*; 2. *Sex*
A **sexy** *sexy, aufreizend, attraktiv*
A **sexual** ['sekʃuəl] *sexuell, Sexual...,*
   Geschlechts...
N **sexuality** [ˌsekʃu'æləti] *Sexualität*
N **sexism** ['seksɪzəm] *Sexismus*
   (= *Diskriminierung von Menschen eines*
   bestimmten Geschlechts, besonders von
   Frauen)
A|N **sexist** ['seksɪst] 1. *sexistisch*;
   2. *Sexist/in*

Collocations with 'sex'

have sex *miteinander schlafen,*
   Geschlechtsverkehr haben
premarital sex [ˌpriː'mærɪtl] / **sex before**
   marriage ['mærɪdʒ] *Sex vor der Ehe*
safe sex *geschützter Sex*
unprotected sex *ungeschützter Sex*
sex education [ˌedʒu'keɪʃn]
   Sexualerziehung, Sexualkunde

German 'Krankheit'

disease [dɪ'ziːz] *eine bestimmte*
   (ansteckende oder ernsthafte) Krankheit
illness *das allgemeine Wort für Krankheit*

CHECKPOINT — *In English, please!*

a *die Geschlechtsreife erreichen / geschlechtsreif werden*
b *Gruppendruck erleben*
c *sexuell aktiv werden*
d *miteinander schlafen, ohne an die Folgen zu denken*

11 **budding sexuality** ['bʌdɪŋ]	*erwachende Sexualität*	N **bud** *Knospe*
12 **sexual maturity** [mə'tʃʊərəti, mə'tjʊərəti]	*Geschlechtsreife*	◊ **immaturity** [ˌɪmə'tjʊərəti] *Unreife* A|V **mature** [mə'tʃʊə] 1. *reif, voll entwickelt;* 2. *reifen* **!** adverb: **sexually mature** *geschlechtsreif*
13 **the emotional side of a relation-ship** [ɪ'məʊʃənl, rɪ'leɪʃnʃɪp]	*die emotionale Seite einer Beziehung*	**be in a relationship** *(von Paar) zusammen sein;* *(von Einzelnem) gebunden sein*
14 **peer pressure** ['pɪə ˌpreʃə]	*Gruppenzwang*	**peer** *(in Schule usw.) Altersgenosse/-in, Gleich-altrige(r)* **give in to / resist peer pressure** [rɪ'zɪst] *dem Gruppenzwang nachgeben/standhalten*
15 **sexually active** [ˌsekʃəli'æktɪv]	*sexuell aktiv*	**!** adverb: **sexually active**
16 **young adult**	*junge(r) Erwachsene(r)*	**young-adult fiction** *Jugendliteratur, Jugendroman*
lose one's **virginity** [və'dʒɪnəti]	*seine Unschuld/Jungfräulichkeit verlieren, zum ersten Mal Sex haben*	N **virgin** ['vɜːdʒɪn] *Jungfrau; jemand, der noch nie Sex hatte*
17 **rite of passage** [raɪt, 'pæsɪdʒ]	*Initiationsritus (= Zeremonie, mit der Jugendliche in die Erwach-senenwelt eingeführt werden)*	**!** homophones: **rite – right – write**
19 **teenage pregnancy** ['pregnənsi]	*Teenagerschwangerschaft*	**pregnancy test** *Schwangerschaftstest* **terminate a pregnancy** ['tɜːmɪneɪt] *einen Schwanger-schaftsabbruch vornehmen* A **pregnant** ['pregnənt] *schwanger*
sexually transmitted disease (abbr. **STD**)	*durch Geschlechtsverkehr übertragene Krankheit, Geschlechtskrankheit*	Examples of sexually transmitted diseases: **AIDS, herpes** ['hɜːpiːz], **syphilis** ['sɪfɪlɪs]

3 Teenage emancipation

20 During adolescence, most young people feel a need to emancipate themselves from their parents. At the same time, that can be very scary: psychologists speak of 'teen angst'. How well someone manages is a question both of upbringing and of personality. The result of the emancipation process is all too
25 often generational conflict, and the generation gap is visible not only at home but at school as well.

Of course teen years are also a time for having fun and experimenting. But many adults have little understanding of youth culture. Whether teens define themselves through
30 fashion, hairstyles, music, playing certain video games or spending time on particular websites, lots of parents and teachers will find something to complain about.

But for every difficult parent-child relationship, there are just as many positive ones in which teens can talk to their parents
35 about anything openly. Studies have shown that a strong relationship with one or both parents can help young people to stay clear of dangerous behaviours such as drug abuse or binge drinking.

Word family 'psychology'

N **psychology** [saɪˈkɒlədʒi] *Psychologie*
N **psychologist** [saɪˈkɒlədʒɪst]
Psychologe/-in
A **psychological** [ˌsaɪkəˈlɒdʒɪkl]
psychisch (Krankheit, Probleme usw.);
psychologisch

Collocations with 'drugs'

be on / take / use drugs *Drogen nehmen*
be addicted to drugs [əˈdɪktɪd] *drogen-*
abhängig sein, drogensüchtig sein
come off / get off drugs
von Drogen loskommen, clean werden

CHECKPOINT — *In English, please!*

a *das Bedürfnis haben, sich von seinen Eltern zu lösen*
b *eine Zeit, in der man Spaß haben und Dinge ausprobieren kann*
c *mit seinen Eltern offen über alles sprechen*
d *gefährliche Verhaltensweisen vermeiden*

20 **adolescence** [ˌædə'lesns]	*Pubertät; Jugend*	= **puberty**
21 **emancipate** oneself **from sb./sth.** [ɪ'mænsɪpeɪt] (fml)	*sich von jdm./etw. emanzipieren*	= **become emancipated from** sb./sth. N **emancipation** [ɪˌmænsɪ'peɪʃn] *Emanzipation*
22 **teen angst** [æŋst]	*Zustand der Angst und Unsicherheit während der Pubertät*	**angst** *Existenzangst, Lebensangst* ❗ *Angst* (allgemein) = **fear** *Angst haben* = **be afraid, be frightened**
23 **upbringing** ['ʌpbrɪŋɪŋ]	*Erziehung*	V **bring** sb. **up** (Kind) *erziehen, großziehen*
25 **generational conflict** [ˌdʒenəreɪʃənl 'kɒnflɪkt]	*Generationskonflikt*	❗ stress: **conflict** ['--] A **intergenerational** *generationsübergreifend, zwischen den Generationen*
the generation gap [ˌdʒenə'reɪʃn gæp]	*die Kluft zwischen den Generationen, der Generationskonflikt*	**gap** *Lücke, Kluft* **gender gap** *Geschlechtsunterschied*
29 **youth culture** ['kʌltʃə]	*Jugendkultur*	❗ stress: **culture** ['--] A **cultural** ['kʌltʃərəl] *kulturell, Kultur...*
define oneself **through sth.** [dɪ'faɪn]	*sich über etw. definieren*	N **definition** [ˌdefɪ'nɪʃn] *Definition*
33 **parent-child relationship** [rɪ'leɪʃnʃɪp]	*Eltern-Kind-Beziehung, Eltern-Kind-Verhältnis*	❗ In noun + noun combinations, the first noun is usually singular in form **(parent)** even if the meaning is plural.
37 **drug abuse** (no pl) ['drʌg_ə,bjuːs]	*Drogenmissbrauch*	**drug** 1. *Droge, Rauschgift;* 2. *Arzneimittel, Medikament* ❗ N **abuse** [ə'bjuːs] – V **abuse** [ə'bjuːz] *missbrauchen*
binge drinking [bɪndʒ]	*übermäßiger Alkoholkonsum, Komasaufen, Kampftrinken*	**binge** (infml) *Sauforgie, Fressorgie*

4 Planning your future

Thinking about the future – what grades one will get in
final exams, what to do after leaving school – is another
important part of growing up. Not everybody has clearly
defined goals and ambitions in life, yet teenagers have to
start making decisions about a career and what kind of
further education they may need.

Lots of young people find that doing a gap year after school
helps them to define their goals, and in some countries there
may be a year or more of military or social service to be done
before those job or university applications have to be written.

Fortunately, the decisions one takes as a teenager needn't be
permanent: in recent years it has become more common –
sometimes even necessary – to switch careers at least once in
one's lifetime.

'Some of these young school-leavers aren't remotely prepared for the realities of the modern work environment.'

No article with 'school'

Do you like school? *Macht dir **die** Schule Spaß?*
start school *in **die** Schule kommen, eingeschult werden*
leave school *von **der** Schule abgehen*
go to school *in **die** Schule / **zur** Schule (= zum Unterricht) gehen*
at school *in **der** Schule (= beim Unterricht)*
after school *nach **der** Schule / Schulzeit*

CHECKPOINT — In English, please!

a *(Schul-)Noten bekommen*
b *klar umrissene Ziele haben*
c *Entscheidungen über den Berufsweg treffen*
d *den Beruf mindestens einmal im Leben wechseln*

39 **grade**	*Zensur, (Schul-)Note*	**grade 1.** (AE) *Klasse, Jahrgangsstufe* (= BE **year**); **2.** (esp. AE) *Note, Zensur* (= BE **mark**)
40 **final exam(ination)** [ˌfaɪnl‿ɪgˈzæm, ɪgˌzæmɪˈneɪʃn]	*Abschlussprüfung*	*das Abitur machen* = **take** one's **school-leaving exams /** (BE also:) **do/take** (one's) **A-levels**
41 **grow up** [ˌ- '-], **grew, grown**	*heranwachsen, aufwachsen; erwachsen werden, groß werden*	A|N **grown-up 1.** *erwachsen;* **2.** *Erwachsene(r)*
42 **goals and ambitions in life** [gəʊlz, æmˈbɪʃnz]	*Lebensziele; Lebensentwurf*	**goal 1.** *Ziel, Plan;* **2.** *Tor* **ambition 1.** *Ehrgeiz;* **2.** *(ehrgeiziges) Ziel, Ambition*
43 **career** [kəˈrɪə]	*(berufliche) Laufbahn, Karriere*	**make a good career for** oneself *Karriere machen*
44 **further education** (no pl, BE) [ˌfɜːðərˌedʒuˈkeɪʃn]	*Weiterbildung, Fortbildung*	**education 1.** *(Schul-, Aus-)Bildung;* **2.** *Erziehung*
45 **gap year** (BE) [gæp]	*Jahr zwischen Schule und Studium oder Beruf*	**take/do a gap year** *ein Jahr aussetzen, eine Auszeit zwischen Schule und Studium nehmen*
46 **define** one's **goals** [dɪˈfaɪn]	*sich eigene Ziele stecken; sich der eigenen Ziele bewusst werden*	**work towards a goal** *auf ein Ziel hinarbeiten* **achieve a goal** [əˈtʃiːv] *ein Ziel erreichen*
47 **military service** [ˈmɪlətri ☆ ˈmɪləteri]	*Wehrdienst*	**do** (one's) **military service** *Wehrdienst (ab)leisten* **compulsory military service** [kəmˈpʌlsəri] *Wehrpflicht*
social service [ˈsəʊʃl]	*Dienst im sozialen Bereich*	*ein Freiwilliges Soziales Jahr (FSJ)* ≈ **a voluntary year of social service**
48 **job application** [ˌæplɪˈkeɪʃn]	*Stellenbewerbung*	V **apply for a job** *sich um eine Stelle bewerben* N **applicant** [ˈæplɪkənt] *Bewerber/in*
university application [ˌjuːnɪˈvɜːsəti]	*Studienbewerbung (bei einer Universität)*	V **apply (to go) to college/university** (BE) N **university applicant** *Studienbewerber/in*

permanent

voluntary
undergo
change
resort to
violence
inferior
democracy

dictatorship
identity
conscious
tribal
discriminate

alternative
lifestyle
social
behaviour
code
motivate

structures
individual
pattern
interact

attitude
aware
social
geographical
self-image

agreement
shift
abide by
constitution

rebel
setting
setting
the rules
species

human
political
well-being
hierarchy

being
structures
thought
circumstances

monarchy
influence
socialize
mainstream

conformity
moral
habit
value
culture

superior
oppose
subculture

The Individual in Society

1   Defined by our environment

2   Shared values and social structures

3   Challenging accepted social structures and values

1 Defined by our environment

Every human being is born into a specific social and geographical setting, e.g. a family, a social class, a country. A child's environment affects how it will think and behave as an adult, and these patterns of thought and behaviour influence
5 an individual's social, cultural, religious and political values, habits and traditions. Both external factors and internal values and habits shape an individual's identity, self-image and well-being.

Human beings are the only species that are aware of their
10 existence, and the fact that people are conscious of their roles within society motivates them to interact with others based on moral values.

'affect' – 'effect'

v **affect** sth. [ə'fekt] *etw. beeinflussen*
N **effect on** sth. [ɪ'fekt] *(Aus-)Wirkung auf etw.*

Word family 'individual'

N **individual** [ˌɪndɪ'vɪdʒuəl] *Einzelperson, Einzelne(r), Individuum*
A **individual** *Einzel..., individuell, persönlich*
N **individuality** [ˌɪndɪˌvɪdʒu'æləti] *Individualität (= Einzigartigkeit der Persönlichkeit)*
N **individualist** [ˌɪndɪ'vɪdʒuəlɪst] *Individualist/in*

CHECKPOINT — *In English, please!*

a *in ein spezifisches soziales und geografisches Umfeld hineingeboren werden*
b *soziale/kulturelle/religiöse/politische/innere/moralische Werte (und Wertvorstellungen)*
c *die Identität eines Individuums prägen*
d *sich seiner Rolle in der Gesellschaft bewusst sein*

1 **human being** [ˌhjuːmən ˈbiːɪŋ]	*Mensch, menschliches Wesen*	= **person**
social and geographical setting [ˈsəʊʃl, ˌdʒiːəˈgræfɪkl]	*sozialer und geografischer Lebensraum, soziales und geografisches Umfeld*	**setting** *Schauplatz, Handlungsort (eines Films usw.)*
4 **pattern of thought and behaviour** [bɪˈheɪvjə]	*Denk- und Verhaltensmuster*	**thought** 1. *Denken, Nachdenken;* 2. *Gedanke* **behaviour** (BE) = **behavior** (AE)
influence sb./sth. [ˈɪnfluəns]	*jdn./etw. beeinflussen*	= **have an influence on sb./sth.** A **influential** [ˌɪnfluˈenʃl] *einflussreich*
5 **values** [ˈvæljuːz]	*Werte, Wertvorstellungen*	V **value** (finanziell) *schätzen; wertschätzen* A **valuable** [ˈvæljuəbl] *wertvoll*
6 **habit** [ˈhæbɪt]	*(An-)Gewohnheit*	**good/bad/annoying habits**
7 **identity** [aɪˈdentəti]	*Identität*	A **identical** [aɪˈdentɪkl] *identisch, gleich* V **identify** [aɪˈdentɪfaɪ] *identifizieren*
self-image [ˌself_ˈɪmɪdʒ]	*Selbstbild*	**have a positive/negative self-image**
8 **well-being** [ˈwelˌbiːɪŋ]	*Wohlergehen*	cf. **I am well** *ich bin gesund; mir geht es gut*
9 **species** [ˈspiːʃiːz] (sing and pl)	*Spezies, (Tier-/Pflanzen-)Art(en)*	**!** pronunciation: **species** [ˈspiːʃiːz]
be aware of sth. [əˈweə] = 10 **be conscious of sth.** [ˈkɒnʃəs]	*sich einer Sache bewusst sein, etw. wissen*	N **awareness** *Bewusstsein, Kenntnis* N **consciousness** *Bewusstsein*
11 **motivate sb. to do sth.** [ˈməʊtɪveɪt]	*jdn. anspornen etw. zu tun, jdn. motivieren etw. zu tun*	N **motivation** [ˌməʊtɪˈveɪʃn] *Motivation, Ansporn* N **motive** [ˈməʊtɪv] *Motiv, Beweggrund*
interact with sb. [ˌɪntərˈækt]	*mit jdm. interagieren, wechselseitig aufeinander einwirken*	N **interaction** *Wechselwirkung, Interaktion* A **interactive** [ˌɪntərˈæktɪv] *interaktiv*
12 **moral** [ˈmɒrəl]	*moralisch*	**!** stress: **moral** [ˈ--] N **morals** (pl) *Moral(vorstellungen)*

2 Shared values and social structures

In order to socialize with others, every individual needs rules by which to abide. These 'rules' or shared values can take many
15 forms, such as family agreements, tribal codes or constitutions.

Social rules change over time and differ according to the values of the culture in which they are made. In the course of history, structures and hierarchies have developed in human society that determine an individual's membership of specific
20 groups, e.g. a class or religion. Democracies, monarchies and dictatorships are some of the social and political structures which exist in the world today.

In a tolerant society, subcultures, made up of like-minded people who reject mainstream culture, may flourish. People
25 also voluntarily join religious communities, political parties or other organizations. A great variety of such institutions helps to shape a healthy democracy.

'member(ship)'
membership of specific groups (AE: **membership** in specific groups)   *Mitgliedschaft **in** bestimmten Gruppen, Zugehörigkeit **zu** bestimmten Gruppen*
be a member of the sports club   *Mitglied **beim/im** Sportverein sein*
a member of society   *ein Mitglied **der** Gesellschaft*
a member of the family   *ein Familienmitglied*

Systems of government
N **democracy** [dɪˈmɒkrəsi] *Demokratie*   A **democratic** [ˌdeməˈkrætɪk] *demokratisch*   N **democrat** [ˈdeməkræt] *Demokrat/in*
N **monarchy** [ˈmɒnəki] *Monarchie*   N **monarch** [ˈmɒnək] *Monarch/in, Herrscher/in*   N **monarchist** [ˈmɒnəkɪst] *Monarchist/in* (= *Anhänger/in der Monarchie*)
N **dictatorship** [dɪkˈteɪtəʃɪp] *Diktatur*   N **dictator** [dɪkˈteɪtə ☆ ˈdɪkteɪtər] *Diktator/in*   A **dictatorial** [ˌdɪktəˈtɔːriəl] *diktatorisch*

CHECKPOINT — *In English, please!*

a *sich im Laufe der Zeit verändern*
b *die Zugehörigkeit eines Individuums zu bestimmten Gruppen festlegen*
c *die Leitkultur ablehnen*
d *freiwillig in eine politische Partei eintreten*

13 **socialize with** sb. ['səʊʃəlaɪz]	*mit jdm. Kontakt pflegen; mit jdm. gesellschaftlich verkehren*	= **mix with** sb. A **social** ['səʊʃl] *sozial; gesellschaftlich* A **sociable** ['səʊʃəbl] *gesellig* N **socialism** ['səʊʃəlɪzəm] *Sozialismus*
rules by which to abide (fml) [ruːlz, ə'baɪd]	*Regeln, nach denen man sich richten muss*	= **rules you have to accept/follow/obey** **abide by** sth. (fml) *sich an etw. halten*
15 **agreement** [ə'griːmənt]	*Vereinbarung*	**reach an agreement** *eine Vereinbarung treffen* V **agree** *sich einigen, vereinbaren*
tribal code [ˌtraɪbl 'kəʊd]	*Stammeskodex (= ungeschriebene Verhaltensregeln, an denen sich ein Stamm orientiert)*	N **tribe** *(Volks-)Stamm* **code 1.** *Kodex* (**code of conduct** *Verhaltensregeln*); **2.** *Code;* **3.** *Vorwahl(nummer)*
constitution [ˌkɒnstɪ'tjuːʃn]	*Verfassung*	A **constitutional** [ˌkɒnstɪ'tjuːʃənl] *verfassungsgemäß, Verfassungs...*
18 **hierarchy** ['haɪərɑːki]	*Hierarchie (= pyramidenförmige Rangordnung)*	❗ stress: <u>hie</u>rarchy ['‑‑‑] A **hierarchical** [ˌhaɪə'rɑːkɪkl] *hierarchisch*
21 **social and political structures** [pə'lɪtɪkl, 'strʌktʃəz]	*soziale und politische Strukturen*	V **structure** *strukturieren, aufbauen* A **structural** ['strʌktʃərəl] *strukturell (bedingt), Struktur...*
23 **subculture** ['sʌbkʌltʃə]	*Subkultur (= Kulturgruppierung innerhalb eines übergeordneten Kulturbereichs)*	**the drug/punk/youth subculture** **culture** ['kʌltʃə] *Kultur* A **cultural** ['kʌltʃərəl] *kulturell, Kultur...*
24 **mainstream culture** ['meɪnstriːm]	*die Leitkultur (der Mehrheit)*	N **the mainstream** *die vorherrschende Richtung*
25 **voluntary** ['vɒləntri ☆ 'vɑːlənteri]	*freiwillig*	◆ **involuntary** *unfreiwillig, gezwungen* N|V **volunteer** [ˌvɒlən'tɪə] **1.** *Freiwillige(r);* **2.** *sich freiwillig melden, ehrenamtlich arbeiten*

3 Challenging accepted social structures and values

If an individual or group feels superior or inferior to other members of society or is discriminated against, this may cause
30 them to alter their attitude towards the accepted social structures. In fact, a shift in popular opinion or external factors like economic, political and environmental circumstances may cause the social structures to undergo permanent change.

If a life of conformity within mainstream culture does not seem
35 possible, people sometimes rebel, e.g. by openly opposing or challenging society's values. If these differences cannot be resolved through discussion and negotiation, people may resort to violence. Some individuals may choose to leave the group and lead an alternative lifestyle, or to join another
40 community which offers them better opportunities.

'I want you to write on the blackboard 100 times: "I will not make fun of a classmate just because he comes from a two-parent family."'

Collocations with 'change'

bring about / cause change
    Veränderungen verursachen/bewirken
trigger change *Veränderungen auslösen*
undergo permanent change ['pɜːmənənt]
    ständige Veränderungen durchmachen/ erfahren
call for / demand change
    Veränderungen fordern/verlangen
oppose/resist change [rɪ'zɪst]
    sich Veränderungen widersetzen
prevent change
    Veränderungen verhindern

CHECKPOINT *In English, please!*

a *sich anderen Mitgliedern der Gesellschaft überlegen fühlen*
b *einen Einzelnen oder eine Gruppe diskriminieren*
c *die gesellschaftlichen Wertvorstellungen infrage stellen*
d *Meinungsverschiedenheiten durch Verhandlungen beilegen*

28	**superior to sb.** [suːˈpɪəriə]	*jdm. überlegen; besser als jd.*	= **better, more powerful or higher in rank than** sb. else N **superiority** [suːˌpɪəriˈɒrəti] *Überlegenheit*
	inferior to sb. [ɪnˈfɪəriə]	*jdm. unterlegen; schlechter als jd.*	= **not as good as** sb. else N **inferiority** [ɪnˌfɪəriˈɒrəti] *Unterlegenheit*
29	**discriminate against sb.** [dɪˈskrɪmɪneɪt]	*jdn. diskriminieren*	**!** discriminate **against** sb. N **discrimination** [dɪˌskrɪmɪˈneɪʃn] *Diskriminierung* A **discriminatory** [dɪˈskrɪmɪnətəri] *diskriminierend*
30	**attitude (to/towards)** [ˈætɪtjuːd]	*Einstellung (zu/gegenüber)*	**have a good/bad/positive/negative attitude to/ towards** sb./sth.
31	**shift**	*Änderung, Wandel; Verschiebung*	**a shift in opinion/policy** V **shift** *verschieben, wechseln*
32	**circumstances** [ˈsɜːkəmstənsɪz]	*Umstände, Verhältnisse*	**economic/political/social circumstances**
34	**conformity** [kənˈfɔːməti]	*Gleichförmigkeit, Anpassung*	V **conform (to** sth.) [kənˈfɔːm] *sich (an etw.) anpassen*
35	**rebel (-ll-)** [rɪˈbel]	*rebellieren, sich auflehnen*	**!** stress: V **rebel** [rɪˈbel] – N **rebel** [ˈrebl] *Rebell/in* N **rebellion** [rɪˈbeljən] *Rebellion, Aufstand*
	oppose sth. [əˈpəʊz]	*gegen etw. sein, sich gegen etw. stellen*	N **opposition** [ˌɒpəˈzɪʃn] *Widerstand, Opposition* N **opponent** [əˈpəʊnənt] *Gegner/in*
38	**resort to violence** [rɪˈzɔːt, ˈvaɪələns]	*Gewalt anwenden, zu Gewalt greifen*	= **turn to / use violence** **!** ing form: **resort to** do**ing** sth. *etw. als letztes Mittel tun (wenn keine andere Wahl bleibt)* A **violent** *gewalttätig, gewaltsam*
39	**an alternative lifestyle** [ɔːlˌtɜːnətɪv ˈlaɪfstaɪl]	*ein alternativer Lebensstil*	**!** stress: al**ter**native [-'---] **lead/live an alternative lifestyle** *alternativ leben* N **alternative** *Alternative*

adopted
ethnic melting
discriminate respect homeland ethnic mix pot ethnic
immigration member of fixed culture multicultural ethnic ghetto
prejudice set of society group society migrant
mix of beliefs segregate shared ethnicity community
cultures national ideas national oath of
nationality swear sense of values voluntarily allegiance
unite character belonging assimilate identity experience
migrant nation politics integrate tradition diversity
population culture stereotype
salad citizen discrimination
bowl identify core immigrant
basic homogeneous social culture embrace
whole group

National Identity and Diversity

1 What is national identity?

National identity, according to a history textbook commonly used in Canada, is 'a sense of, and pride in, the character of one's nation'. It is the sum total of a country's culture and traditions, its language or languages, and its politics.

5 Most people identify with the country they were born in and have at least a vague notion of what that nation stands for. Although people's definitions of their country's identity may be different, there is usually a good deal of overlap.

But what exactly is 'the character of one's nation'? Most
10 attempts to define a country's national character end up with nothing but a list of stereotypes. These fixed ideas of what people in a particular country are like may have some basis in fact, but they are often wrong when applied to individuals.

CHECKPOINT ← *In English, please!*

a *Stolz auf die eigene Nation*
b *sich mit dem Land identifizieren, in dem man geboren ist*
c *zumindest eine vage Vorstellung davon haben, wofür das Land steht*
d *nichts als eine Aufzählung von Klischees*

Collocations with 'national'

national identity cf. p. 33
national character cf. p. 33
national anthem ['ænθəm]
    Nationalhymne
national currency *Landeswährung*
national dish *Nationalgericht*
national flag *Nationalflagge*
national holiday *Nationalfeiertag*
national language *Landessprache*
national park *Nationalpark*
national service *Wehrdienst*
national team *Nationalmannschaft*
National Socialism *der National-sozialismus*

German 'Politik'

politics ['pɒlətɪks] **1.** *politisches Leben / Geschehen;* **2.** *politische Ansichten*
- **Are you interested in politics?**
- **Her politics are quite radical.**

policy ['pɒləsi] *politische Maßnahmen, Linie*
- **the Government's foreign policy**
- **a new policy on education**

1 **national identity** [ˌnæʃnəl_aɪˈdentəti]	*nationale Identität*	❗ pronunciation: **national** [ˈnæʃnəl] – **nation** [ˈneɪʃn] *Nation, Volk* stress: **identity** [-ˈ---] **cultural/social/personal/group identity**
3 **culture** [ˈkʌltʃə]	*Kultur*	❗ stress: **culture** [ˈ--] No article: **in Western/European/African/Islamic culture** A **cultural** [ˈkʌltʃərəl] *kulturell, Kultur...* A **(un)cultured** *(un)kultiviert, (un)gebildet* (Person)
4 **tradition** [trəˈdɪʃn]	*Tradition*	**by tradition** *nach altem Brauch, traditionsgemäß* A **traditional** [trəˈdɪʃənl] *traditionell*
5 **identify with** sth. [aɪˈdentifaɪ]	*sich mit etw. identifizieren*	**identify** sb. *jdn. identifizieren* **identify** oneself *sich ausweisen* N **identification** [aɪˌdentɪfɪˈkeɪʃn] **1.** *Identifizierung;* **2.** *Ausweis*
10 **national character** [ˈkærəktə]	*Nationalcharakter; Volks- charakter*	❗ stress: **character** [ˈ---] A|N **characteristic** [ˌkærəktəˈrɪstɪk] **1.** *charakteristisch, typisch* (**of** *für*); **2.** *charakteristisches Merkmal, typische Eigenschaft* N **characterization** [ˌkærəktəraɪˈzeɪʃn] *Charakterisierung, Beschreibung*
11 **stereotype** [ˈsteriətaɪp]	*Stereotyp; Klischee(vorstellung)*	**a common/traditional/negative stereotype** **cultural/gender/racial stereotypes**
fixed ideas (often disapproving)	*feste Vorstellungen*	**have fixed ideas/opinions about/of** sth. *feste (unveränderbare) Vorstellungen von / Meinungen über etw. haben*

2 Unity

National identity is really a question of shared values which
15 give the different ethnic and social groups within a society a
sense of belonging.

In Western societies, principles such as the belief in a representative democracy and equality before the law serve to unite a nation. New members of society are expected to accept
20 that basic set of beliefs, to obey the laws of their host country and to respect its culture. And if they wish to become citizens of their adopted homeland, they usually have to swear an oath of allegiance to their new country.

An 1889 cartoon portraying the American melting pot (cf. p.36)

CHECKPOINT ⟨ *In English, please!*

a der Glaube an eine repräsentative Demokratie
b Prinzipien wie Gleichheit vor dem Gesetz
c von neuen Mitgliedern erwarten, dass sie sich an die Gesetze ihres Gastlandes halten
d einen Treueeid auf seine neue Heimat schwören

Collocations with 'ethnic' ['eθnɪk]

ethnic group *ethnische Gruppe* (= Volksgruppe mit einheitlicher Kultur- und Lebensgemeinschaft), Ethnie
ethnic minority [maɪˈnɒrəti] *ethnische Minderheit*
ethnic identity *ethnische Identität*
ethnic tensions ['tenʃnz] *Spannungen zwischen ethnischen Gruppen*
ethnic violence *Gewalt zwischen ethnischen Gruppen*

14 **shared values** [ˌʃeəd ˈvæljuːz]	*gemeinsame Wertvorstellungen*	◆ **conflicting values** V **value** (*finanziell*) *schätzen; wertschätzen* A **valuable** [ˈvæljuəbl] *wertvoll*
15 **social group** [ˈsəʊʃl]	*soziale Gruppe*	**social class/background**
16 **sense of belonging** [bɪˈlɒŋɪŋ]	*Zugehörigkeitsgefühl*	◆ **sense of not belonging / sense of exclusion**
18 **unite a nation** [juˈnaɪt, ˈneɪʃn]	*eine Nation (ver)einen, eine Nation verbinden*	A **united** *vereinigt, vereint* N **unity** [ˈjuːnəti] *Einheit*
19 **member of society** [səˈsaɪəti]	*Mitglied der Gesellschaft, Teil der Gesellschaft*	! *Ich bin Mitglied im/beim Sportverein.* = **I am a member of the sports club.** No article: **in Western/today's/German society**
20 **basic set of beliefs** [bɪˈliːfs]	*grundsätzliche Überzeugungen, Grundannahmen*	**belief 1.** *Glaube* (**his belief in** God); **2.** *Überzeugung* V **believe** [bɪˈliːv] *glauben*
21 **respect a culture** [rɪˈspekt]	*eine Kultur respektieren*	N **respect** *Respekt, Achtung*
22 **citizen** [ˈsɪtɪzn]	*Staatsangehörige(r); Bürger/in*	**become a German citizen** *die deutsche Staatsbürgerschaft erhalten* N **citizenship** *Staatsbürgerschaft, Staatsangehörigkeit*
adopted homeland [əˈdɒptɪd]	*Wahlheimat*	= **adopted country** **adopt** *adoptieren, annehmen* **adopted child** *Adoptivkind*
23 **swear an oath of allegiance** [sweə, ˌəʊθ_əv_əˈliːdʒəns], **swore, sworn**	*einen Treueschwur leisten*	= **take an oath of allegiance** **swear 1.** *schwören;* **2.** *fluchen* **oath** *Eid, Schwur* **allegiance** (**to** sb./sth.) *Treue (zu jdm./etw.), Loyalität (gegenüber jdm./etw.)*

3 Cultural diversity

Nationality has little to do with ethnicity: even countries which
25 have only recently had significant numbers of immigrants
have always had an ethnic mix.

As a result of immigration, most countries have become – if they
weren't already – multicultural societies. Diversity is an accepted
fact. Although some immigrants experience prejudice and
30 discrimination, most integrate into the core culture successfully. That does not necessarily mean that they have had to
assimilate, giving up their original national or ethnic identities.

On the contrary, today it is generally accepted that a society
benefits from a mix of cultures. Whereas the USA, for example,
35 was once viewed as the great 'melting pot' in which differences
were melted down to create a homogeneous whole, Americans
today often describe their society as a 'salad bowl' with distinct
parts that, together, make up an interesting and successful
whole.

Word family 'immigrate'

v **immigrate** ['ɪmɪgreɪt]
einwandern, immigrieren
n **immigrant** ['ɪmɪgrənt]
Einwanderer/Einwanderin
n **immigration** [ˌɪmɪ'greɪʃn]
Einwanderung, Immigration

Word family 'emigrate'

v **emigrate** ['emɪgreɪt]
auswandern, emigrieren
n **emigrant** ['emɪgrənt]
Auswanderer/Auswanderin
n **emigration** [ˌemɪ'greɪʃn]
Auswanderung, Emigration

CHECKPOINT *In English, please!*

a *als Folge von Immigration; aufgrund von Zuwanderung*
b *von einer kulturellen Mischung profitieren*
c *die USA als den großen „Schmelztiegel" betrachten*
d *unterschiedliche Teile, die eine gelungene Einheit (= ein erfolgreiches Ganzes) bilden*

24	**nationality** [ˌnæʃəˈnæləti]	*Staatsangehörigkeit, Nationalität*	**dual nationality** *doppelte Staatangehörigkeit* A|N **national** **1.** *national;* **2.** *Staatsangehörige(r)* A|N **nationalist** [ˈnæʃnəlɪst] **1.** *nationalistisch;* **2.** *Nationalist/in*
	ethnicity [eθˈnɪsəti]	*ethnische Zugehörigkeit, Volks-zugehörigkeit*	A **ethnic** [ˈeθnɪk] *ethnisch*
26	**an ethnic mix**	*eine ethnische Mischung/Viel-falt, eine ethnisch gemischte Bevölkerung*	V **mix** *(sich) mischen, (sich) vermischen*
28	**a multicultural society** [ˌmʌltiˈkʌltʃərəl]	*eine multikulturelle Gesellschaft*	**multi...** (prefix) = **more than one; many**
	diversity [daɪˈvɜːsəti]	*Vielfalt, Verschiedenheit*	A **diverse** [daɪˈvɜːs] *verschieden, unterschiedlich*
29	**experience prejudice and discrimination** [ɪkˈspɪəriəns, ˈpredʒudɪs, dɪˌskrɪmɪˈneɪʃn]	*Vorurteilen und Diskriminierung begegnen*	N **experience** *Erfahrung, Erlebnis* ! pronunciation: **prejudice** [ˈpredʒudɪs] A **be prejudiced** *Vorurteile haben*
30	**integrate into the core culture** [ˈɪntɪgreɪt]	*sich in die Kernkultur/Leitkultur integrieren*	N **integration** [ˌɪntɪˈgreɪʃn] *Integration* **core** *Kern(gehäuse); innerer Kern*
32	**assimilate** [əˈsɪməleɪt]	*sich anpassen, sich angleichen*	**assimilate into/to the community** N **assimilation** [əˌsɪməˈleɪʃn] *Aufnahme, Integration*
34	**a mix of cultures**	*eine kulturelle Mischung/Vielfalt*	= **a cultural mix**
35	**melting pot** [ˈ-- -]	*Schmelztiegel*	V **melt** *(zer)schmelzen, sich auflösen*
36	**a homogeneous whole** (fml) [ˌhɒməˌdʒiːniəs ˈhəʊl]	*ein einheitliches Ganzes*	**homogeneous** *homogen, gleichartig* ◑ **heterogeneous** [ˌhetərəˈdʒiːniəs] *heterogen*
37	**salad bowl** [ˈsæləd bəʊl]	*Salatschüssel*	! **bowl** [bəʊl] *Schüssel* – **bowel** [ˈbaʊəl] *Darm*

4 Immigration and integration

40 Countries that have failed to grasp the advantages of diversity or to embrace immigration have often found that their migrant populations do not integrate. Instead, migrants have either voluntarily segregated themselves or have been discriminated against and thus forced into ethnic ghettos in 45 large cities. Whatever the reasons, it is clear that this is not in the interests of the migrants or of society as a whole; debate over the best way to integrate migrant communities continues.

'Now, don't make a big fuss – we're just migrant workers.'

Verbs used with or without a direct object

integrate/assimilate immigrants into the community *Immigranten in die Gemeinschaft integrieren*

Immigrants *integrate/assimilate* into the community. *Immigranten integrieren **sich** in die Gemeinschaft.*

change the make-up of the population *die Zusammensetzung der Bevölkerung verändern*

The make-up of the population *changes*. *Die Zusammensetzung der Bevölkerung verändert **sich**.*

CHECKPOINT *In English, please!*

a *die Chancen der Vielfalt nicht begreifen*
b *Migranten diskriminieren*
c *Migranten in ethnische Großstadtgettos drängen*
d *nicht im Interesse der Migranten sein*

41 **embrace immigration** [ɪmˈbreɪs] (fml)	(die) Immigration annehmen/akzeptieren	**embrace** (fml) *umarmen*
42 **migrant population** [ˌmaɪɡrənt ˈpɒpjuleɪʃn]	aus Zuwanderern bestehende Bevölkerungsgruppe	❗ pronunciation: **migrant** [ˈmaɪɡrənt] **migrant** *Migrant/in, Zu- oder Abwanderer/-in, Umsiedler/in* **migrant worker** *Wanderarbeiter/in, Zuwanderer/-in* **economic migrant** *Wirtschaftsflüchtling* v **migrate** [maɪˈɡreɪt ☆ ˈmaɪɡreɪt] *(ab)wandern* N **migration** *Migration, (Ab-)Wanderung* v **populate** [ˈpɒpjuleɪt] *bevölkern, besiedeln*
43 **voluntarily segregate** oneself [ˈvɒləntrəli ☆ ˌvɑːlənˈterəli, ˈseɡrɪɡeɪt] (fml)	sich freiwillig abspalten	◑ **involuntarily** *unfreiwillig, gezwungenermaßen* A **voluntary** *freiwillig* N **segregation** [ˌseɡrɪˈɡeɪʃn] *Trennung* **racial segregation** [ˈreɪʃl] *Rassentrennung* ◑ **racial integration**
44 **discriminate against** sb. [dɪˈskrɪmɪneɪt]	jdn. diskriminieren, jdn. benachteiligen	❗ **discriminate against** sb. *die Diskriminierung von Ausländern =* N **discrimination against** foreigners A **discriminatory** [dɪˈskrɪmɪnətəri ☆ dɪˈskrɪmɪnətɔːri] *diskriminierend*
ethnic ghetto [ˈɡetəʊ], pl **ghettos** or **ghettoes**	Getto, in dem ausschließlich Angehörige einer ethnischen Gruppe leben	
47 **migrant community** [kəˈmjuːnəti]	Gemeinschaft von Einwanderern, Migrantengemeinschaft	A **common** *gemeinsam*

 # The United Kingdom

1 An economic, military and cultural force

The United Kingdom of Great Britain and Northern Ireland is made up of four countries or 'national regions' located on the British Isles at Europe's north-western edge. As an island nation, the UK has developed separately from the rest of Europe.

5 Once the world's most powerful country with an empire that spanned the globe, the United Kingdom is still a force to be reckoned with.

The UK has one of the largest economies in the world. Its voice is heard internationally because it is a permanent member of

10 the United Nations Security Council. As a NATO member with its own nuclear arsenal and highly respected armed forces, the UK is also a major military power.

Additionally, the UK exerts tremendous influence on culture in the western world, acting as a trendsetter in art, music and

15 fashion as well as in other areas of popular culture.

GB

MARTIN GUHL

Tricky pronunciations

island ['aɪlənd] *Insel*
Ireland ['aɪələnd] *Irland*
Iceland ['aɪslənd] *Island*
the British Isles [aɪlz] *die Britischen Inseln*
Eire ['eərə] *die Republik Irland*

German 'Sicherheit'

security [sɪ'kjʊərəti] *(innere/äußere) Sicherheit, Sicherheitsvorkehrungen*
- **public/social/financial security**
- **job security**

safety *das Sichersein vor Gefahr*
- **safety at work**
- **safety measure** ['meʒə]

CHECKPOINT — *In English, please!*

a *aus vier Ländern bestehen*
b *sich unabhängig vom übrigen Europa entwickeln*
c *eine Kraft sein, mit der man rechnen muss*
d *enormen Einfluss auf die Kultur der westlichen Welt ausüben*

2 **national region** [ˌnæʃnəl ˈriːdʒən]	*Staatsregion, in der eine Nation lebt (z. B. Wales oder Schottland)*	N **nation** [ˈneɪʃn] *Nation, Volk* ❗ pronunciation: **region** [ˈriːdʒən]
3 **island nation** [ˌaɪlənd ˈneɪʃn]	*Inselstaat*	
5 **empire** [ˈempaɪə]	*Imperium; Kaiserreich*	**the British Empire** *das Britische Weltreich* N **emperor** [ˈempərə] / **empress** [ˈemprəs] *Kaiser/in*
9 **a permanent member** [ˈpɜːmənənt]	*ein ständiges Mitglied*	◀▶ **a non-permanent member** ❗ stress: **permanent** [ˈ– – –]
10 **the United Nations Security Council** [sɪˈkjʊərəti ˌkaʊnsl]	*der Sicherheitsrat der Vereinten Nationen, der UN-Sicherheitsrat*	cf. GET THE CONTEXT, p. 99 ❗ homophones: **council – counsel** *Rat(schlag)*
11 **nuclear arsenal** [ˌnjuːkliər ˈɑːsənl]	*Kernwaffenarsenal*	❗ stress: **arsenal** [ˈ– – –]
the armed forces (pl) [ˌɑːmd ˈfɔːsɪz]	*die Streitkräfte, das Militär*	V **arm** *(sich) bewaffnen* N **arms** (pl, fml) *Waffen*

GET THE CONTEXT

1 **Great Britain**, consisting of England, Wales and Scotland

2 **The United Kingdom of Great Britain and Northern Ireland**

3 **The British Isles**, consisting of the UK and the Republic of Ireland (Eire)

2 Government

With its long history the UK has many **time-honoured traditions**. The UK is **a constitutional monarchy** and even has an **established church**, i.e. an official state religion, **the Church of England**, with the **monarch** at its head. (The Archbishop of Canterbury
20 runs the day-to-day affairs of the Church.) The monarch has no real power and is said to **reign**, not **rule**.

Actual power is in the hands of **the Government** – **the Prime Minister** and **Cabinet** – and **Parliament**. Parliament itself consists of two houses. **The lower house**, **the House of Commons**, is
25 **elected** by the people. Members of **the upper house**, **the House of Lords**, are either **appointed** because of past service to the nation ('life peers') or have **inherited** their seats ('hereditary peers').

CHECKPOINT — *In English, please!*

a *sich um das Alltagsgeschäft der Anglikanischen Kirche kümmern*
b *aus einem Unterhaus und einem Oberhaus bestehen*
c *vom Volk gewählt werden*
d *jemanden ernennen aufgrund seiner früheren Verdienste um das Land*

■ **the Prime Minister (PM)** [ˌpraɪm ˈmɪnɪstə] *der/die Premierminister/in*
- head of the government
- leader of the strongest party in the House of Commons

■ **the Cabinet** [ˈkæbɪnət] *das Kabinett, der Ministerrat*
- about 20 of the most important Ministers (heads of government departments)

■ **the House of Commons** [ˈkɒmənz] (also called **the lower house** *das Unterhaus*)
- 650 MPs from constituencies
- makes laws
- elected for each constituency in a first-past-the-post system
- elections are held at least every five years

■ **the House of Lords** (also called **the Lords** or **the upper house** *das Oberhaus*)
- ca. 830 members (life peers, 26 Anglican bishops, and 92 hereditary peers)
- scrutinizes bills passed by the House of Commons

16 **a time-honoured tradition** ['taɪm_ˌɒnəd trə'dɪʃn]	*eine althergebrachte Tradition; eine altehrwürdige Tradition*	v|n **honour** (BE) = **honor** (AE) **1.** *ehren;* **2.** *Ehre*
17 **a constitutional monarchy** [ˌkɒnstɪtjuːʃənl 'mɒnəki]	*eine konstitutionelle Monarchie (in der die Macht des Königs / der Königin durch eine Verfassung eingeschränkt wird)*	n **constitution** [ˌkɒnstɪ'tjuːʃn] *Verfassung* **!** pronunciation: **mon**archy ['mɒnə**ki**]
established church [ɪ'stæblɪʃt]	*Staatskirche*	= **state church**
18 **the Church of England**	*die anglikanische Kirche*	= **the Anglican Church** ['æŋglɪkən]
19 **monarch** ['mɒnək ☆ 'mɑːnərk]	*Monarch/in; Herrscher/in*	n **monarchy** *Monarchie*
the Archbishop of Canterbury [ˌɑːtʃ'bɪʃəp, 'kæntəbri]	*der Erzbischof von Canterbury*	= **the head of the Church of England**
21 **reign** [reɪn]	*herrschen, Herrscher/in sein*	n **reign** *Herrschaft, Regentschaft*
rule (a country) [ruːl]	*(über ein Land) herrschen, (ein Land) regieren*	n **rule** *Herrschaft* n **ruler** *Herrscher/in*
22 **the Government** ['gʌvənmənt]	*die Regierung*	v **govern** *regieren*
23 **Parliament** ['pɑːləmənt]	*das britische Parlament*	**!** stress and spelling: **parl**iament ['pɑːləmənt]
25 **elect** sb. [ɪ'lekt]	*jdn. wählen*	**elect** sb. **(as) MP** *jdn. zum Abgeordneten wählen* n **election** [ɪ'lekʃn] *Wahl*
26 **appoint** sb. [ə'pɔɪnt]	*jdn. ernennen*	**appoint** sb. **(as) president** *jdn. zum Präsidenten ernennen* n **appointment** *Ernennung (zu einem Amt)*
27 **inherit** sth. [ɪn'herɪt]	*etw. erben*	n **inheritance** [ɪn'herɪtəns] *Erbe, Vermögen* n **heir** [eə] / **heiress** ['eəres] *Erbe/Erbin* A **hereditary** [hə'redɪtri ☆ -teri] *Erb..., erblich*

3 Constitution

The UK has no written constitution. Instead, the 'constitution'
consists of a body of laws and legal precedent. In recent years,
the constitution has undergone huge changes. For example,
much of the country's legislative power has been devolved
from the UK Parliament to the Scottish Parliament and to
national assemblies in Wales and Northern Ireland. England did
not get its own parliament under devolution; it is still governed
by the national Parliament.

In 2009 a Supreme Court was established as a final court of
appeal and constitutional court; until then those powers were
exercised within the House of Lords.

The Lords itself may soon be subject to constitutional reform: for
the first time ever there is general agreement that the upper
house should become an elected body, although discussion of
its exact structure may go on for quite some time.

The Supreme Court

The separation of powers

legislative power [ˈledʒɪslətɪv ☆ -leɪtɪv]
gesetzgebende Gewalt, Legislative
executive power [ɪgˈzekjətɪv]
*vollziehende/vollstreckende Gewalt,
Exekutive*
judicial power [dʒuˈdɪʃl]
richterliche Gewalt, Judikative

Collocations with 'court'

in court *vor Gericht* (**!** **at court** *bei Hofe*)
go to court *vor Gericht gehen*
take sb. **to court** *jdn. verklagen*

CHECKPOINT — *In English, please!*

a *aus einer Sammlung von*
   Rechtsvorschriften bestehen
b *grundlegende Änderungen erfahren*

c *Befugnisse im Oberhaus ausüben*
d *einer Verfassungsreform*
   unterzogen werden

29 **a written constitution** [ˌkɒnstɪˈtjuːʃn]	eine schriftliche Verfassung, eine geschriebene Verfassung	◀▶ **an unwritten constitution** A **constitutional** verfassungsgemäß, Verfassungs...
30 **legal precedent** [ˌliːgl ˈpresɪdənt]	richtungsweisende Gerichts-entscheide; rechtlicher Präzedenzfall (= früherer Fall, Beispielsfall)	❗ pronunciation: **legal** [ˈliːgl] **precedent** [ˈpresɪdənt] – **president** [ˈprezɪdənt] – **precedence** [ˈpresɪdəns] Vorrang A **unprecedented** [ʌnˈpresɪdentɪd] beispiellos, noch nie da gewesen
32 **legislative power has been devolved** [dɪˈvɒlvd]	die Legislative wurde auf lokale Ebene übertragen	**devolve power** Macht dezentralisieren/übertragen/verlagern
33 **the Scottish Parliament**	das schottische Parlament	❗ spelling: N **Scotland** – A **Scottish** schottischer Whisky = **Scotch Whisky**
34 **national assembly** [ˌnæʃnəl_əˈsembli]	Nationalversammlung, Parlament	**assembly** 1. (politische) Versammlung; 2. morgendliche Schulversammlung; 3. Montage, Zusammenbau
35 **devolution** [ˌdiːvəˈluːʃn]	Dezentralisierung; Machtüber-tragung	V **devolve** [dɪˈvɒlv] (Macht) übertragen
37 **Supreme Court** [suːˌpriːm ˈkɔːt]	Oberster Gerichtshof	= **High Court** **court** 1. Gericht; 2. (Königs-)Hof
court of appeal, pl **courts of appeal** [əˈpiːl]	Berufungsgericht, Berufungs-instanz	**final court of appeal** oberstes Berufungsgericht N|V **appeal** 1. Berufung, Einspruch; 2. Berufung einlegen, Einspruch erheben
38 **constitutional court** [ˌkɒnstɪˈtjuːʃnl]	Verfassungsgericht	N **constitution** Verfassung
40 **constitutional reform** [rɪˈfɔːm]	Verfassungsreform	V **reform** reformieren
42 **an elected body** [ɪˈlektɪd]	ein gewähltes Gremium	**body** 1. Körper; 2. Körperschaft, Gremium

4   School system and social status

The school system in the UK has been reformed many times in
45 recent years. A national curriculum has been introduced in
England, Wales and Northern Ireland with course requirements
that are meant to standardize education, eliminate inequalities
and improve schools by forcing them to compete with one
another. The effectiveness of the curriculum, however, is continu-
50 ally in dispute.

But neither changes to the school system, where 90% of pupils
attend comprehensive schools, nor political reforms can hide the
fact that the UK is still far from being a classless society. In the
past, people's social status depended on having the 'right' accent
55 or attending the 'right' schools. While this is no longer the case,
a young person's career chances still depend to a large extent on
how much money their family has or who their parents know.
In this sense the UK is more like other western societies.

Word family 'equal'

A **equal** ['iːkwəl] *gleich*
A **unequal** *ungleich*
N **equal** *Gleichgestellte(r)*
V **equal** *gleichkommen, gleichen*
N **equality** [iˈkwɒləti] *Gleichheit,*
    Gleichberechtigung
N **inequality** [ˌɪnɪˈkwɒləti] *Ungleichheit*

German 'Schüler/in'

pupil (BE, starting to become old-
    fashioned) = **a child in a school**
schoolboy/schoolgirl/schoolchild
    = **a boy/girl/child who attends school**
student ['stjuːdənt] = **a person studying**
    at a school, college, university, etc.

CHECKPOINT *In English, please!*

a *Schulen zwingen, miteinander zu konkurrieren*
b *weit davon entfernt sein, eine klassenlose Gesellschaft zu sein*
c *in hohem Maß davon abhängen, wie viel Geld die Familie eines jungen*
    Menschen hat

44 **school system** ['sɪstəm]	*Schulsystem, Schulwesen*	**!** stress: **system** ['--]
46 **course requirements** ['kɔːs rɪ‚kwaɪəmənts]	*Kursanforderungen, Lehrplan-forderungen*	v **require** [rɪ'kwaɪə] *erfordern, verlangen*
47 **standardize education** [‚stændədaɪz _‚edʒu'keɪʃn]	*die Ausbildung vereinheitlichen, das Bildungswesen standardi-sieren*	n **standard** ['stændəd] *Standard, Norm, Maßstab* v **educate** ['edʒukeɪt] *ausbilden, unterrichten* A **educational** [‚edʒu'keɪʃənl] *Bildungs...*
eliminate inequalities [ɪ'lɪmɪneɪt]	*Ungleichheiten aus der Welt schaffen*	= **remove or get rid of inequalities** n **elimination** [ɪ‚lɪmɪ'neɪʃn] *Beseitigung, Eliminierung*
52 **attend** (fml) **a comprehensive school** [ə'tend, ‚kɒmprɪ'hensɪv]	*eine Gesamtschule besuchen, auf eine Gesamtschule gehen*	= **go to a comprehensive school** n **attendance** [ə'tendəns] *Anwesenheit; Schulbesuch*
a political reform [pə‚lɪtɪkl rɪ'fɔːm]	*eine politische Reform*	n **politics** ['pɒlətɪks] *Politik* v **reform** *reformieren*
53 **a classless society** [sə'saɪəti]	*eine klassenlose Gesellschaft*	◀▶ **a class society**
54 **social status** (usu. sing) ['steɪtəs]	*gesellschaftliche Stellung*	**marital status** ['mærɪtl] (fml) *Familienstand*
56 **career chance** [kə'rɪə]	*Berufschance, Karriere-möglichkeit*	**make a good/successful career for** oneself *Karriere machen*

GET THE CONTEXT

■ **the national curriculum** [kə'rɪkjələm] *der landesweite zentrale Lehrplan* (in Großbritannien) All state schools in England, Wales and Northern Ireland follow the national curriculum which is divided into four so-called **Key Stages**. Pupils are tested after each stage: at ages 7, 11 and 14. At 16 they take the **General Certificate of Secondary Education (GCSE)** in several subjects, and at 18 those who have stayed on at school take their **A-levels**.

The United States of America

1 The American dream

The American dream may mean different things to different people, but the basic idea is that anybody can achieve anything, no matter how great the odds are against him or her. Most Americans believe that, with a strong will and hard work, anybody can go 'from rags to riches', or that anybody can become the president of what they consider to be 'the greatest country on earth'.

Some would claim that the men who later became known as the 'Founding Fathers' were themselves dreamers. They believed, for example, that it was possible to run a country on the principles of personal liberty, self-government and individual rights. In the Declaration of Independence (1776) they wrote that 'all men are created equal' and had 'inalienable rights' such as 'life, liberty and the pursuit of happiness'. This last idea became central to the American dream.

CHECKPOINT — *In English, please!*

a *für verschiedene Menschen Unterschiedliches bedeuten*
b *Jeder kann alles erreichen.*
c *die USA für „das großartigste Land der Welt" halten*
d *ein Land auf der Grundlage des Prinzips persönlicher Freiheit regieren*

GET THE CONTEXT

■ **An excerpt from the Declaration of Independence (1776)**
[ˌdeklə'reɪʃn, ˌɪndɪ'pendəns]
die Unabhängigkeitserklärung der Vereinigten Staaten von Amerika

We hold these truths to be self-evident, that all men are created equal, that they are endowed by their Creator with certain unalienable Rights, that among these are Life, Liberty and the pursuit of Happiness. That to secure these rights, Governments are instituted among Men, deriving their just powers from the consent of the governed.
That whenever any Form of Government becomes destructive of these ends, it is the Right of the People to alter or to abolish it, and to institute new Government, laying its foundation on such principles and organizing its powers in such form, as to them shall seem most likely to effect their Safety and Happiness.

1 **the American dream**	*der amerikanische Traum*	v **dream** *träumen* N **dreamer** *Träumer/in*
3 **The odds are against him.** [ɒdz]	*Seine Chancen stehen schlecht.*	**odds** (pl) *Aussichten, (Gewinn-)Chancen*
4 **hard work**	*harte/anstrengende Arbeit*	◊ **easy/light work** *leichte Arbeit* v **work** *arbeiten*
5 **from rags to riches** ['rɪtʃɪz]	*vom Tellerwäscher zum Millionär*	**rags** (pl) *Lumpen* **riches** (pl) *Reichtümer*
8 **the Founding Fathers** [ˌfaʊndɪŋ 'fɑːðəz]	*die Gründungsväter (= die Mitglieder der verfassungs- gebenden Versammlung der USA von 1787, z.B. George Washington, Thomas Jefferson und Benjamin Franklin)*	v **found** *gründen* N **foundation 1.** *Gründung;* **2.** *Stiftung*
11 **personal liberty** [ˌpɜːsənl 'lɪbəti]	*persönliche Freiheit*	= **personal freedom**
self-government ['gʌvənmənt]	*Selbstverwaltung*	v **govern** *regieren*
individual rights [ˌɪndɪ'vɪdʒuəl]	*individuelle Rechte, Rechte des Einzelnen*	N **individual** *Individuum, Einzelne(r)* **civil rights** ['sɪvl] *(Staats-)Bürgerrechte* **human rights** ['hjuːmən] *Menschenrechte* **animal rights** *Rechte der Tiere* **equal rights** ['iːkwəl] *Gleichberechtigung*
13 **inalienable rights** [ɪn'eɪliənəbl] (fml)	*unabdingbare Rechte, unver- äußerliche Rechte*	! **Inalienable** usually comes <u>before</u> a noun.
14 **the pursuit of happiness** [pə'sjuːt ☆ pər'suːt]	*das Streben nach Glück*	v **pursue** [pə'sjuː] **1.** *verfolgen, erreichen wollen;* **2.** *(einem Studium, Hobby usw.) nachgehen*

2 The US Constitution

After the War of Independence the Founders drafted the US Constitution (1787), which established a government with three separate and independent branches that watch over one another. This system of checks and balances is supposed to prevent any one branch from becoming too powerful – a serious worry for the Framers of the Constitution after fighting a war against a king who had, they felt, abused his power.

The Capitol (where Congress meets)

16	**the US Constitution** [ˌkɒnstɪ'tju:ʃn]	*die Verfassung der USA*	A **constitutional** [ˌkɒnstɪ'tju:ʃənl] *verfassungsgemäß, Verfassungs...* A **unconstitutional** *verfassungswidrig*
18	**separate and independent branches** ['seprət, 'brɑːntʃɪz]	*einzelne und unabhängige Staatsgewalten*	❗ A **separate** ['seprət] – V **separate** ['sepəreɪt] **branch** 1. *Zweig, Ast;* 2. *Sparte, Zweig;* 3. *Zweigstelle*
21	**the Framers of the Constitution**	*die Verfasser/Autoren der Verfassung der USA*	V **frame** (fml) *entwickeln, gestalten; formulieren*
22	**abuse one's power** [ə'bju:z]	*seine Macht missbrauchen*	N **abuse** [ə'bju:s] **of power** *Machtmissbrauch*
▪	**electorate** [ɪ'lektərət]	*Wähler(schaft)*	V **elect** *wählen* N **election** [ɪ'lekʃn] *Wahl*
▪	**the executive branch** [ɪg'zekjətɪv]	*die Exekutive*	= **the executive**
▪	**the legislative branch** ['ledʒɪslətɪv ☆ 'ledʒɪsleɪtɪv]	*die Legislative*	= **the legislature** ['ledʒɪsleɪtʃə] (fml) N **legislation** [ˌledʒɪs'leɪʃn] *Gesetze, Gesetzgebung*
▪	**the judicial branch** [dʒu'dɪʃl]	*die Judikative*	= **the judiciary** [dʒu'dɪʃəri ☆ dʒu'dɪʃieri]
▪	**approve** sth. [ə'pru:v]	*(Maßnahmen usw.) genehmigen*	N **approval** [ə'pru:vl] *Zustimmung, Genehmigung*
▪	**appointment** [ə'pɔɪntmənt]	*Ernennung (zu einem Amt)*	**appointment** 1. *Verabredung, Termin (beim Arzt usw.);* 2. *Ernennung* V **appoint** sb. *jdn. ernennen, einstellen*
▪	**impeach** sb. [ɪm'pi:tʃ]	*gegen jdn. ein (Amtsenthebungs-)Verfahren einleiten*	N **impeachment** *Anklage wegen eines Vergehens im Amt*
▪	**veto** sth. (vetoes, vetoing, vetoed) ['vi:təʊ]	*sein Veto gegen etw. einlegen*	❗ pronunciation: **veto** ['vi:təʊ] N **veto** *Veto*
▪	**propose** sth. [prə'pəʊz]	*etw. vorschlagen*	N **proposal** [prə'pəʊzl] *Vorschlag*
▪	**confirm** sth. [kən'fɜ:m]	*etw. bestätigen*	N **confirmation** [ˌkɒnfə'meɪʃn] *Bestätigung*

3   Individual rights and freedoms

Once the Constitution had been ratified (i.e. accepted by the necessary number of states), a Bill of Rights (1791) was drawn
25 up to ensure the individual rights and freedoms of American citizens by limiting the power of the government. One thing the government cannot do, for example, is establish a state religion. Although the separation of church and state is central to American freedoms, religion tends to play a huge role not only
30 in Americans' daily lives, but also in their politics: it is hard to imagine that someone who does not believe in God could ever be elected President.

The rights and freedoms mentioned in the Declaration of Independence and the Bill of Rights did not always apply to
35 everyone. Native Americans first became US citizens in 1924, and black people did not achieve full legal equality until the Civil Rights Movement finally forced change in the mid-1960s. And although many Americans like to speak of a 'post-racial society' following the election of the nation's first black president in
40 2008, discrimination is still a fact of life for many non-white Americans.

Collocations with 'right of'

right of assembly *Versammlungsrecht*
right of asylum *Asylrecht, Recht auf Asyl*
right of citizenship *Staatsbürgerrecht*
right of free speech *Recht der freien Meinungsäußerung*
right of ownership *Eigentumsrecht, Besitzrecht*

Collocations with 'freedom of'

freedom of the press *Pressefreiheit*
freedom of expression *Meinungsfreiheit*
freedom of speech *Redefreiheit*
freedom of religion = religious freedom *Religionsfreiheit*
freedom of information *Informationsfreiheit*
freedom of movement *Bewegungsfreiheit*

CHECKPOINT — *In English, please!*

a *eine Charta der Grundrechte erstellen*
b *die Individualrechte amerikanischer Bürger garantieren*
c *an Gott glauben*
d *jemanden zum Präsidenten wählen*

23 **ratify** sth. ['rætɪfaɪ]	(einen Vertrag) *ratifizieren, in Kraft setzen*	N **ratification** [ˌrætɪfɪˈkeɪʃn] *Ratifizierung*
24 **Bill of Rights**	*(Charta der) Grundrechte der amerikanischen Bürger/innen*	= the first ten **amendments** *(Zusatzartikel)* to the US **Constitution**
25 **freedom** ['friːdəm]	*Freiheit*	= **liberty** A **free** *frei* ! *Frieden* = **peace**
26 **citizen** ['sɪtɪzn]	*Bürger/in*	N **citizenship** *Staatsbürgerschaft, Staatsangehörigkeit*
limit the power of the government ['lɪmɪt]	*die Macht der Regierung beschränken/begrenzen*	N **limit** *Begrenzung* V **govern** *regieren*
28 **the separation of church and state** [ˌsepəˈreɪʃn]	*die Trennung von Kirche und Staat*	V **separate** ['sepəreɪt] *trennen* A **separate** ['seprət] *getrennt*
34 **apply to** sb./sth. [əˈplaɪ]	*für jdn./etw. gelten, auf jdn./etw. zutreffen*	! *sich um eine Stelle bewerben* = **apply for** a job
36 **achieve full legal equality** [əˈtʃiːv, ˌliːgl iˈkwɒləti]	*die volle juristische Gleichberechtigung erreichen*	N **achievement** *Leistung; Errungenschaft* A **equal** ['iːkwəl] *gleich*
the Civil Rights Movement [ˌsɪvl ˈraɪts]	*die (amerikanische) Bürgerrechtsbewegung*	**civil** *(staats)bürgerlich, Bürger...*
38 **a post-racial society** [ˌpəʊst ˌreɪʃl səˈsaɪəti]	*eine Gesellschaft, in der die Zugehörigkeit zu einer ethnischen Gruppe keine Rolle mehr spielt*	**post-...** (prefix) *nach..., Nach...* **racial** *Rassen..., ethnisch* N **race** *ethnische Gruppe, Rasse*
39 **election** [ɪˈlekʃn]	*Wahl*	V **elect** *wählen*
40 **discrimination** [dɪˌskrɪmɪˈneɪʃn]	*Diskriminierung*	! *jdn. diskriminieren* = **discriminate against** sb.

4   The American way of life

Since Americans are so convinced that their form of government is the best, they have often tried to export it, whether by military or by economic means. As **the sole remaining superpower**, <u>the US</u> is the object of much envy and hatred around the world.

Anti-American sentiment is widespread, but <u>America</u> is also much admired. All over the world, young people listen to American music, watch American films, use American products and imitate **the American way of life**. They, too, want their piece of the American dream.

'I was looking for my piece of the American dream when I bought this truck … now I'm looking for a parking space.'

'the United States' / 'the USA' / 'the US' + singular verb

The United States *has* reacted angrily.
The USA *consists* of 50 states.
<u>The US</u> *is* the object of much envy.

'America' – 'the US'

<u>America</u> (= the US) is much admired.
The use of 'America' to mean just 'the US' is very common, but many people from other parts of the American continent dislike it.

CHECKPOINT   *In English, please!*

a *eine Regierungsform mit militärischen Mitteln exportieren*
b *viel Neid und Hass auf sich ziehen*
c *ein Stück vom amerikanischen Traum abhaben wollen*

44 **the sole remaining superpower** [rɪ'meɪnɪŋ]	*die einzige verbleibende Super-macht*	= **the only superpower left** **sole** *einzige(r, s), alleinige(r, s)* v **remain** *(ver)bleiben, übrig bleiben*
46 **anti-American sentiment** (fml) ['ænti, 'sentɪmənt]	*antiamerikanische Stimmung*	**anti-...** (prefix) *anti..., gegen... eingestellt; Anti..., Gegen...* ! stress: <u>sen</u>timent ['---] **public sentiment** *die öffentliche Meinung*
49 **the American way of life**	*die amerikanische Art zu leben, die amerikanische Lebensweise/ Lebensform*	

TYPICAL RIVALRY
IDENTIFY WARM TRADITIONAL THRIFT
RESIDENT GENEROUS
MAIN COVER DISPLAY COUNTY LUSH
PRIDE HISTORICAL TIES FEATURE BOUNDARY
GEOGRAPHICAL ENCOMPASS
LANDSCAPE TRADITION REGIONAL
PLENTIFUL CHARACTERISTIC POLITICAL LOYALTY
HARSH BE KNOWN CLIMATE REGION LAND
AREA CELTIC RUGGED BOND HARVEST
SPECIALITY FRINGE CROP TOGETHER LANGUAGE
HANDICRAFTS DIALECT CONFLICT NEIGHBOURING
REGIONALISM

Regions of the UK and the USA

1 What is a region?

A 'region' can be an area defined by political boundaries, or it can be larger or smaller, encompassing a group of countries or a tiny corner of a single county within a country.

In many cases a region is defined by a feature of the landscape.
5 Such a geographical region can be relatively small, e.g. the Lake District, 2300 sq km of lakes and moors in Cumbria in the northwest of England; or it can be huge, e.g. the Great Plains of North America, which cover some 1.3 million sq km in west central USA and Canada.

10 Many regions are defined by history. East Anglia in the United Kingdom, named after an Anglo-Saxon kingdom that ended about 1000 years ago, or the American South, which consists for the most part of the Southern states that tried to leave the Union during the American Civil War of 1861–1865, are
15 examples of historical regions.

CHECKPOINT — *In English, please!*

a *sich über eine Fläche von rund 1,3 Millionen Quadratkilometern erstrecken*
b *nach einem angelsächsischen Königreich benannt sein*
c *größtenteils aus den Südstaaten bestehen*

German 'Grenze'

boundary *die Grenze eines Grundstücks, Parks oder Feldes; die Grenze eines kommunalen oder regionalen Verwaltungsbezirks*
border *die Grenzlinie zwischen Staaten*
limit *Begrenzung, Beschränkung*

'county' – 'country'

county ['kaʊnti] *Grafschaft (in Groß-britannien, Irland); Verwaltungsbezirk, Landkreis (in den USA)*
country ['kʌntri] *Land, Staat*

German 'Landschaft'

landscape *natürliche oder von Menschen geschaffene Landschaft*
countryside *Gegend, Natur*
scenery ['siːnəri] *schöne Landschaft / Gegend*

The pronunciation of 'south'

the American South [saʊθ]
the Southern ['sʌðən] **states**
Southerners ['sʌðənəz] (p. 64)
southerly ['sʌðəli] **winds**

1	**a political boundary** ['baʊndri]	*eine politische Grenze*	**boundary changes** *Grenzänderungen* **boundary disputes** *Grenzstreitigkeiten*
2	**encompass sth.** [ɪnˈkʌmpəs] (fml)	*etw. umfassen, etw. umschließen*	= **include** sth.
4	**a feature of the landscape** [ˈfiːtʃə, ˈlændskeɪp]	*ein Merkmal der Landschaft*	= **a characteristic of the landscape**
5	**a geographical region** [ˌdʒiːəˈɡræfɪkl ˈriːdʒən]	*eine (geografische) Region*	N **geography** [dʒiˈɒɡrəfi] *Geografie, Erdkunde* ❗ pronunciation: **region** [ˈriːdʒən] A **regional** [ˈriːdʒənl] *regional, Regional...*
8	**cover an area** [ˈkʌvə]	*sich über ein Gebiet erstrecken, ein bestimmtes Gebiet umfassen*	= **spread over an area**
15	**a historical region** [hɪˈstɒrɪkl]	*eine historische Region*	N **history** *Geschichte*

GET THE CONTEXT

■ **geographical regions**

The Lake District

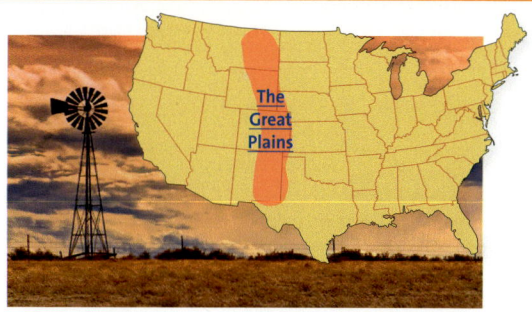

The Great Plains

2 Typical characteristics

The people of a region often display certain characteristics that are considered 'typical' of that region. In the UK the Scots, for example, are known for their thrift; in the USA Southerners are highly regarded for their hospitality.

20 Did the rugged landscape of Scotland, with its harsh climate, where it is hard to grow most crops, result in thrift? Did the lush land and warm climate of the American South, where harvests are plentiful, simply allow people to be more generous? It is a matter of speculation whether their respective regions 25 made them that way, or whether certain personalities are drawn to particular regions.

CHECKPOINT *In English, please!*

a *bestimmte Merkmale einer Region für typisch halten*
b *wegen seiner Gastfreundschaft sehr geschätzt werden*
c *zu Sparsamkeit führen / Sparsamkeit zur Folge haben*
d *Darüber lässt sich nur spekulieren. / Das ist reine Spekulation.*

16 **display certain characteristics** [dɪˈspleɪ, ˌkærəktəˈrɪstɪks]	*bestimmte Merkmale aufweisen*	N **display 1.** *Vorführung, Demonstration;* **2.** *Anzeige (auf einem Bildschirm)*
17 **typical** [ˈtɪpɪkl]	*typisch*	◊ **untypical/atypical** [ˌeɪˈtɪpɪkl] *untypisch/atypisch* ❗ *typisch für* = **typical of** *typisch deutsch* = **typically** German N **type** [taɪp] *Typ*
18 **be known for** sth. [nəʊn]	*für/wegen etw. bekannt sein*	**well known / well-known** *(wohl)bekannt*
thrift	*Sparsamkeit*	A **thrifty** *sparsam* ❗ *sparsam sein* = **be careful with money** *mit etw. sparsam umgehen, etw. sparsam* *verwenden* = **be economical with** sth., **use** sth. **sparingly, go easy on** sth. (infml)
20 **rugged landscape** [ˈrʌgɪd]	*wilde/schroffe/felsige Land- schaft*	❗ pronunciation: **rugged** [ˈrʌgɪd] N **ruggedness** *Wildheit/Schroffheit (der Landschaft)*
21 **crop** (often pl **crops**)	*Feldfrucht, Ernte(ertrag)*	**grow/plant crops** *Feldfrüchte anbauen* **a heavy/poor crop** *eine reiche/schlechte Ernte, ein hoher/niedriger Ertrag*
22 **lush land** [lʌʃ]	*üppiges Land, saftiges (Gras-) Land*	**lush 1.** *saftig;* **2.** *schön, luxuriös* N **lushness** *Saftigkeit, Üppigkeit (der Vegetation)*
23 **a plentiful harvest** [ˌplentɪfl ˈhɑːvɪst]	*eine reiche Ernte*	= **a good/rich harvest** ◊ **a bad/poor harvest** N **plenty** (fml) *Überfluss* PRON **plenty of ...** *viel(e) ...* V **harvest** *ernten*
generous [ˈdʒenərəs]	*großzügig, freigebig*	◊ **mean** *geizig* N **generosity** [ˌdʒenəˈrɒsəti] *Großzügigkeit*

3   Language

The residents of a region sometimes speak their own language, as is the case with some people on the so-called Celtic fringe. These are regions where a Celtic language was spoken recently 30 or in some cases still is spoken in everyday life: Scotland, Wales, Northern Ireland and Cornwall in the UK, the Republic of Ireland, the Isle of Man between the islands of Great Britain and Ireland, and Britanny in the northwest of France.

More often, though, the people of a region speak a regional 35 dialect, which bonds them together and makes outsiders more easily identifiable. Even where regional languages and dialects are spoken, today all their speakers also speak their country's main language.

'dialect' – 'accent'
(regional) dialect ['daɪəlekt] *Dialekt, Mundart, regionale Variante einer Sprache* (die sich von anderen Varianten in Bezug auf Aussprache, Wortwahl und teilweise auch Grammatik unterscheidet)
■ **the Yorkshire dialect**

accent ['æksent, 'æksənt] *(regionaler) Akzent, (regionale) Aussprachevariante*
■ **a strong/broad accent** *ein starker Akzent*
■ **speak with an Indian / a Scottish accent**
■ **speak without an accent** *akzentfrei sprechen*

Collocations with 'language'

first/native language
  Erst-/Muttersprache
foreign/second language
  Fremd-/Zweitsprache
official language [ə'fɪʃl] *Amtssprache*
main language *Hauptsprache, vorherrschende Sprache*
national language *Landessprache*
regional language *Regionalsprache*
sign language [saɪn] *Zeichensprache*

CHECKPOINT   *In English, please!*

a *Nordirland*
b *die Republik Irland*
c *die Inseln Großbritannien und Irland*
d *die Bretagne im Nordwesten Frankreichs*

27 **resident** ['rezɪdənt]	Bewohner/in, Einheimische(r)	V **reside** [rɪ'zaɪd] (fml) *seinen Wohnsitz haben* N **residence** ['rezɪdəns] (fml) *Wohnsitz, Residenz* A **residential** [ˌrezɪ'denʃl] *Wohn...*
28 **the Celtic fringe** [ˌkeltɪk 'frɪndʒ]	die keltische Randzone (= die Regionen, in denen keltische Sprachen gesprochen werden)	N **the Celts** [kelts] *die Kelten* **fringe** *Rand (eines Gebiets oder Bezirks)*
35 **bond** sb./sth. **together** [bɒnd]	jdn./etw. zusammenschweißen	N **bond (between A and B / with C)** *Bindung (zwischen A und B / an C)*

GET THE CONTEXT

■ the Celtic fringe

Scotland
Northern Ireland
the Isle of Man
Wales
the Republic of Ireland
Cornwall
Britanny

'Bill, in the country it's a CELLAR, not a BASEMENT!
I won't come down 'til you use the proper term.'

4 Regional identity

Whether a region is a product of history, geography or simply
40 tradition, the residents of a region generally identify with their
region and feel pride in and loyalty to their region. A person's
regional ties are often stronger than their bond with their
country and can be expressed in many different ways.

Whereas past wars have been fought because of regionalism,
45 today it is most often expressed through regional rivalries,
especially in the area of sport and usually between neighbouring
regions.

There can, of course, be bitter rivalry between regions, but most
of it is good-natured, as when the English tell jokes about the
50 Scots. Indeed humour is one common way of dealing with
regional conflict; as a rule, regionalism is embraced.

We take great delight in traditional handicrafts of a specific
region and even travel to enjoy regional specialities, be it
rattlesnake in the Southwest or clam chowder on the east coast
55 of the USA, haggis in Scotland, Caerphilly cheese in Wales or
cream tea in Cornwall in the UK.

Collocations with 'regional'

regional ties (pl) [taɪz] *regionale
  Bindungen; regionale Anbindungen*
regional rivalry ['raɪvlrɪ]
  Rivalität zwischen Regionen
regional conflict ['kɒnflɪkt] *regionaler
  Konflikt, regionale Konflikte, Streitig-
  keiten zwischen (den) Regionen*
regional speciality [ˌspeʃɪ'ælətɪ] (BE)
  *regionale Spezialität, landestypische
  Spezialität*
regional language *Regionalsprache*

'Scot' – 'Scottish'

**The Scots / The Scottish tell jokes about
  the English.** *(Die) Schotten erzählen …*
He's Scottish / a Scot. *Er ist Schotte.*
! *schottischer Whisky* = **Scotch whisky**

CHECKPOINT *In English, please!*

a *sich mit seiner Region identifizieren*
b *Rivalitäten im Bereich des Sports*
c *eine häufige Form des Umgangs mit
   regionalen Konflikten*
d *große Freude an der traditionellen
   Handwerkskunst einer bestimmten
   Gegend haben*

40 **tradition** [trəˈdɪʃn]	*Tradition, Brauch*	A **traditional** [trəˈdɪʃnl] *traditionell*
identify with sth. [aɪˈdentɪfaɪ]	*sich mit etw. identifizieren, sich mit etw. verbunden fühlen*	**identify** sb. *jdn. identifizieren* **identify** oneself *sich ausweisen* N **identification** [aɪˌdentɪfɪˈkeɪʃn] **1.** *Identifizierung;* **2.** *Ausweis*
41 **pride in** sth. [praɪd]	*Stolz auf etw.*	! **take pride in** sth. = **be proud of** sth. *stolz auf etw. sein*
loyalty to sth./sb. [ˈlɔɪəlti]	*Treue zu etw./jdm.*	A **loyal** [ˈlɔɪəl] *treu, loyal*
44 **regionalism** [ˈriːdʒənəlɪzəm]	*Regionalismus*	= **1.** *Streben einer Region nach größerer politischer und wirtschaftlicher Unabhängigkeit;* **2.** *regionale Spracheigentümlichkeiten*
46 **a neighbouring region** [ˈneɪbərɪŋ]	*eine angrenzende Region*	**neighbouring** (BE) = **neighboring** (AE) N **neighbour** (BE) = **neighbor** (AE) *Nachbar/in*
52 **traditional handicrafts** (usu. pl) [ˈhændɪkrɑːfts]	*traditionelle Handarbeiten, traditionelles Kunstgewerbe*	**handicraft** (AE also: **handcraft**) *Handfertigkeit; (Kunst-)Handwerk*

GET THE CONTEXT

■ **regional specialties**

rattlesnake *(Klapper-schlange)* from the South-west of the USA

clam chowder *(Muschel-suppe)* from the east coast of the USA

haggis *(mit Innereien gefüllter Schafsmagen)* from Scotland

Caerphilly [kəˈfɪli] **cheese** from Wales

cream tea (a light meal of scones with jam and cream) from England

Urban, Suburban and Rural Lifestyles

1 Urbanization

In Britain, cities began growing rapidly in the second half of the 18th century as a result of the Industrial Revolution. Agricultural reform pushed the poor off the land and into the rapidly growing centres of manufacture in search of work.

5 Before the invention of the steam locomotive, cities developed along water transport lines; thus the early American centres of population, like most European cities, were located at the coast or along rivers.

It was not until the age of the railway that cities could
10 develop independently of water transport. In the USA, rapid industrialization increased the pace of urbanization. Today 77 per cent of Americans are classified by the U.S. Census Bureau as 'urban'.

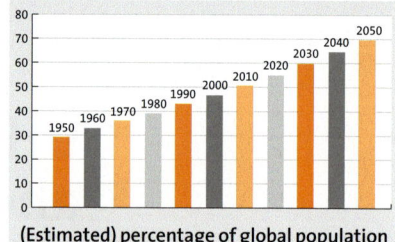

(Estimated) percentage of global population living in urban areas

CHECKPOINT — *In English, please!*

a *Die Städte wuchsen infolge der industriellen Revolution.*
b *Die Armen waren auf der Suche nach Arbeit.*
c *Erst im Zeitalter der Eisenbahn konnten sich die Städte entwickeln.*
d *Die rasante Industrialisierung erhöhte das Tempo der Urbanisierung.*

The railway

railway (BE) = **railroad** (AE) *(Eisen-)Bahn*
railway line (BE) = **1. railroad track** (AE) *Bahntrasse, Gleis*; **2. railroad line** (AE) *Bahnlinie*
railway station (BE) = **railroad station** (AE) = **train station** *Bahnhof*
go/travel by rail = **go/travel by train** *mit der Bahn fahren/reisen*

locomotive [ˌləʊkəˈməʊtɪv] *Lokomotive* = **(railway) engine** [ˈendʒɪn]
steam/diesel/electric locomotive *Dampf-/Diesel-/Elektrolok(omotive)*

1 **grow rapidly** ['ræpɪdli]**, grew, grown**	*schnell (an)wachsen*	N **(rapid) growth** *(schnelles) Wachstum*
2 **the Industrial Revolution** [ɪn,dʌstriəl ,revə'lu:ʃn]	*die industrielle Revolution*	A|N **revolutionary** [,revə'lu:ʃənəri ☆ -neri] **1.** *revolutionär;* **2.** *Revolutionär/in* V **revolutionize** [,revə'lu:ʃənaɪz] *revolutionieren*
3 **agricultural reform** [,ægrɪkʌltʃərəl rɪ'fɔ:m]	*Agrarreform(en), landwirtschaftliche Reform(en)*	N **agriculture** ['ægrɪkʌltʃə] *Landwirtschaft* V **reform** *reformieren*
6 **water transport** ['trænspɔ:t]	*Wassertransport; Transport auf dem Wasserweg, Schiffsverkehr*	**!** stress: <u>**trans**port</u> ['--] **transport** (BE) = **transportation** (AE) **air/freight/road transport** V **trans**<u>**port**</u> [-'-] *transportieren, befördern*
centre of population [,pɒpju'leɪʃn]	*Bevölkerungszentrum, Ballungsraum*	**centre** (BE) = **center** (AE) V **populate** ['pɒpjuleɪt] *bevölkern, besiedeln*
7 **be located** [ləʊ'keɪtɪd ☆ 'loʊkeɪtɪd]	*sich befinden, liegen*	= **be situated** ['sɪtʃueɪtɪd] V **locate** *ausfindig machen, orten* N **location** *Lage, Standort*
11 **industrialization** [ɪn,dʌstriəlaɪ'zeɪʃn]	*Industrialisierung*	A **industrial** [ɪn'dʌstriəl] *industriell, Industrie...* V **industrialize** [ɪn'dʌstriəlaɪz] *industrialisieren* N **industrialist** [ɪn'dʌstriəlɪst] *Industrielle(r)* N **industry** ['ɪndəstri] *Industrie*
urbanization [,ɜ:bənaɪ'zeɪʃn]	*Verstädterung, Urbanisierung*	A **urbanized** ['ɜ:bənaɪzd] *verstädtert, urbanisiert* A **urban** ['ɜ:bən] *städtisch, Stadt...; urban* ◊ **rural** ['rʊərəl] *ländlich*
12 **census** ['sensəs]	*(Volks-)Zählung, Zensus*	**the U.S. Census Bureau** *die US-amerikanische Statistikbehörde, das Statistische Bundesamt der USA*

2 Suburbanization and surrounding towns

After World War II, <u>urban growth</u> in the USA was mainly driven
by <u>suburbanization</u>, set in motion by federal and state <u>policies</u>
and made possible by rapid motorization, low house
construction costs and the availability of cheap land for
<u>residential areas</u>. This migration of former city dwellers to the
outskirts of cities resulted in a number of problems: the
separation of residence and workplace led to considerable traffic
congestion and air pollution as the private car became the main
means of transport. The suburban landscape became dominated
by the car, with drive-in facilities ranging from fast-food
restaurants to drive-in banks, drive-in cinemas and even drive-in
churches.

In the UK, town planning laws prohibited such excesses, but the
high cost of <u>urban life</u> drove many middle-class <u>residents</u> out of
the urban centres to surrounding towns, where housing was
cheaper and the quality of life better.

CHECKPOINT — *In English, please!*

a *etwas in Gang setzen*
b *etwas ermöglichen / etwas möglich machen*
c *zu einer Reihe von Problemen führen*

Collocations with 'urban'

urban area *Stadtgebiet, städtischer Raum*
urban centre *städtisches Zentrum*
<u>**urban growth**</u> *Städtewachstum*
<u>**urban life**</u> *Stadtleben, das Leben in der Stadt*
urban development *Stadtentwicklung*
urban renewal *Stadterneuerung*
urban dweller *Stadtbewohner/in*

German 'Politik'

policy ['pɒləsi] *politische Maßnahmen, politische Linie, gesetzliche Bestimmung*
■ **the Government's foreign policy**
■ **a new policy on education**

politics ['pɒlətɪks] **1.** *politisches Leben / Geschehen;* **2.** *politische Ansichten*
■ **Are you interested in politics?**
■ **Her politics are quite radical.**

Word family 'resident'

N <u>**resident**</u> ['rezɪdənt] *Bewohner/in, Einwohner/in, Einheimische(r)*
A **resident** *wohnhaft, ansässig*
A **residential** [ˌrezɪ'denʃl] *Wohn...*
   <u>**residential area**</u> *Wohngebiet*
N **residence** ['rezɪdəns] (fml) **1.** *Wohnsitz, Residenz;* **2.** *Aufenthalt* (in einem Land)

15 **suburbanization** [sə,bɜːbənaɪˈzeɪʃn]	*Suburbanisation (= Ausdehnung der Großstädte durch Angliederung von Vororten und Trabantenstädten), Stadtflucht*	A **suburban** [səˈbɜːbən] *Vorort..., Vorstadt...* N **suburb** [ˈsʌbɜːb] *Vorort* **live in the suburbs** *am Stadtrand wohnen*
16 **motorization** [ˌməʊtəraɪˈzeɪʃn]	*Motorisierung*	N **motor** [ˈməʊtə] *Motor*
17 **availability** [əˌveɪləˈbɪləti]	*Verfügbarkeit*	A **available** [əˈveɪləbl] *verfügbar, erhältlich*
18 **migration** [maɪˈɡreɪʃn]	*(Zu-/Ab-/Aus-)Wanderung, Zug*	V **migrate** [maɪˈɡreɪt ☆ ˈmaɪɡreɪt] *(fort)ziehen, (ab-/aus)wandern*
city dweller	*Stadtbewohner/in*	= **urban dweller** V **dwell** (fml), **dwelt, dwelt** = **live** N **dwelling** (fml) *Wohnung, Wohnsitz*
outskirts (pl) [ˈaʊtskɜːts]	*Stadtrand, Vorort*	! **on the outskirts of Berlin** *am Stadtrand von Berlin*
20 **traffic congestion** [kənˈdʒestʃən]	*Verkehrsstau*	= **traffic jam** A **congested** [kənˈdʒestɪd] **1.** *verstopft* (Straßen); **2.** *überfüllt, übervölkert* (**congested area** *Ballungsgebiet*)
air pollution [pəˈluːʃn]	*Luftverschmutzung*	V **pollute** [pəˈluːt] *verschmutzen* N **polluter** *Umweltverschmutzer/in, -sünder/in*
22 **means of transport,** pl **means of transport** [ˈtrænspɔːt]	*Transportmittel, Verkehrsmittel*	**public transport** (BE) = **public transportation** (AE) *öffentliche Verkehrsmittel*
23 **drive-in facility** [fəˈsɪləti]	*Drive-in-Anlage*	! stress: <u>**drive**-in</u> [ˈ--]
26 **town planning laws** [lɔːz]	*Baugesetze, Planungsrecht*	= **urban planning laws**
28 **housing** (no pl) [ˈhaʊzɪŋ]	*Unterkunft, Wohnungen*	= **houses, flats/apartments** ! **house** [haʊs] – **houses** [ˈhaʊzɪz] – **housing** [ˈhaʊzɪŋ]

3 City and suburbs

30 With more and more residents migrating to the suburbs, the deserted parts of US inner cities were increasingly occupied by low-income ethnic populations, leading to the growth of slums and ghettos. The exodus of high-income residents meant a loss of tax revenue. The cities were now burdened with the problem of masses of people streaming in and out every day and little
35 money to maintain the necessary infrastructure. Inner-city ghettos became plagued by crime, poverty and racial conflict.

The pressure on upwardly mobile families to escape to the safety of the suburbs grew, and by the 1960s mainstream American
40 culture had become suburban culture. At the same time, the geographic expansion of urban centres, together with major highway construction, ended the isolation that had characterized rural life for centuries.

Many families move to the suburbs in search of more space.

CHECKPOINT — *In English, please!*

a *an den Stadtrand ziehen*
b *die erforderliche Infrastruktur unterhalten*
c *von Armut geplagt sein / unter Armut leiden*
d *in die Sicherheit der Vororte entfliehen*

Hyphenated compound expressions before nouns	
a low income	low-income housing
a high income	high-income residents
inner cities	inner-city ghettos
the middle class	a middle-class suburb
fast food	a fast-food restaurant

31 **deserted** [dɪˈzɜːtɪd]	*verlassen, unbewohnt*	= **abandoned** [əˈbændənd] v **desert** *verlassen, im Stich lassen* ❗ v de**sert** [dɪˈzɜːt] *verlassen* N **des**ert [ˈdezət] *Wüste* N des**sert** [dɪˈzɜːt] *Nachtisch, Dessert*
inner city	*Innenstadt (= meist herunter-gekommene Viertel mit sozialen Problemen usw.)*	❗ *Innenstadt (= Stadtzentrum, City)* = **town/city centre** (BE); ADV|A|N **downtown** (AE)
32 **slum** [slʌm]	*Slum, Elendsviertel*	**city/urban slums** *Slums der Großstädte, städtische Elendsviertel*
33 **ghetto** [ˈɡetəʊ], pl **-os** or **-oes**	*Getto, Armenviertel*	**ethnic/immigrant/racial ghettos**
exodus (sing) [ˈeksədəs] (fml)	*Abwanderung, Auswanderung, Exodus*	◄► **(mass) arrival** *(massenhafte) Ankunft, Masseneinwanderung*
a loss of tax revenue [ˈrevənjuː ☆ -nuː]	*ein Steuerausfall, ein verringertes Steueraufkommen*	v **lose** [luːz], **lost, lost** *verlieren* N|v **tax** 1. *Steuer;* 2. *besteuern* **revenue** *Staatseinnahmen, -einkünfte*
36 **infrastructure** [ˈɪnfrəstrʌktʃə]	*Infrastruktur*	A **infrastructural** [ˌɪnfrəˈstrʌktʃərəl] *die Infrastruktur betreffend, infrastrukturell*
38 **upwardly mobile** [ˌʌpwədli ˈməʊbaɪl ☆ ˈməʊbl]	*hier: sozial aufstiegsfähig*	A **upward** *Aufwärts...* N **upward mobility** [məʊˈbɪləti] *soziale Aufstiegsfähigkeit*
41 **the expansion of urban centres** [ɪkˈspænʃn]	*die Erweiterung/Ausdehnung urbaner Zentren*	= **the growth of urban centres** N **expanse** [ɪkˈspæns] *Weite, Fläche* v **expand** *(sich) ausdehnen, expandieren* **centre** (BE) = **center** (AE)

4 Return to the city

Beginning in the mid-1970s, a <u>revitalization</u> of American inner
cities took place as a wave of **investment** saw new hotels and
businesses created. Moreover, it became fashionable for young
affluent professionals to buy and renovate architecturally
interesting buildings in formerly run-down neighbourhoods, a
process referred to as '**gentrification**'. To the growing numbers
of **yuppies**, who were mostly childless and single, living close to
the city centres with all their **amenities** became more attractive.
Rising **commuting costs** have provided a further **incentive** for
people to return to the city.

'Let's face the facts, Walter – we've become
middle-aged *urban professionals*.'

CHECKPOINT — *In English, please!*

a *architektonisch interessante Gebäude*
b *ehemals heruntergekommene Gegenden*
c *ein als Gentrifizierung bezeichneter Prozess*
d *die steigende Zahl von zumeist kinderlosen und unverheiraten Yuppies*
e *steigende Fahrtkosten zum Arbeitsplatz*

45 **investment** [ɪn'vestmənt]	*Investition(en)*	**encourage foreign investment** *ausländische Investitionen fördern* v **invest** [ɪn'vest] *investieren, (Geld) anlegen* N **investor** [ɪn'vestə] *Investor/in, Kapitalanleger/in*
47 **affluent** (fml) ['æfluənt]	*wohlhabend, reich*	= **prosperous** ['prɒspərəs], **wealthy** ['welθi] **affluent society** *Wohlstandsgesellschaft, Überflussgesellschaft* N **affluence** ['æfluəns] *Überfluss, Wohlstand*
professional [prə'feʃənl]	*in einem gehobenen Beruf Tätige(r), Akademiker/in; qualifizierte(r) Berufstätige(r)*	A **professional 1.** *beruflich, Berufs...;* **2.** *professionell, fachmännisch;* **3.** *in einem gehobenen Beruf tätig* N **profession** [prə'feʃn] *akademischer Beruf*
49 **gentrification** [ˌdʒentrɪfɪ'keɪʃn]	*soziale Umstrukturierung einer Wohngegend, Aufwertung, Gentrifizierung*	v **gentrify** ['dʒentrɪfaɪ] *(Gegend) aufwerten (durch Renovierungsarbeiten, Zuzug von sozial Bessergestellten usw.)*
50 **yuppie** ['jʌpi] (infml) **= young urban professional**	*Yuppie, Angehörige(r) der städtischen oberen Mittelschicht*	= **yuppy**
51 **amenities** (usu. pl) [ə'mi:nətiz ☆ ə'menətiz]	*Vorzüge, Annehmlichkeiten (eines Hauses), Freizeiteinrichtungen (einer Stadt)*	= **features that make a place comfortable or easy to live in** **have all the amenities / be close to all the amenities**
52 **commuting costs** [kə'mju:tɪŋ]	*Fahrtkosten (für den täglichen Weg zur Arbeit)*	v|N **commute 1.** *(mit dem Auto, Zug usw.) pendeln;* **2.** *Arbeitsweg, tägliche Fahrt zwischen Arbeit und Zuhause* N **commuter** *(Berufs-)Pendler/in*
incentive [ɪn'sentɪv]	*Anreiz, Ansporn*	◊ **disincentive** *Entmutigung, Abschreckung* **an incentive for** sb. **to do sth.**

goods

manufacturing

Hindu

middle class

expand

economic

service industry

information

technology Sectarian

superpower

live birth

nuclear violence

infrastructure

colonial

weapons

parliamentary

power presence

democracy

billion System of

jewel in

grow workforce

sanitation

Hindi overpopulated

cover

the crown

independence

British

government

colonial

poverty

slum

access

movement census

subcontinent

period

call centre

nuclear

Empire

Partition

infant

literacy rate

power

life

colony

of India

mortality

expectancy

cheap

diarrhoea

Raj

labour

India

1 Contrasts

2 Colonial past and its consequences

3 Economic advances

4 A booming job market

1 Contrasts

India is a <u>land</u> of contrasts. It is a <u>country</u> where traditions from thousands of years ago live alongside some of the 21st century's most advanced technology. It is home to one third of the world's poorest people and to over 126,000 dollar millionaires and around 50 billionaires. It has a parliamentary system of government and is the world's largest democracy, but at the same time millions of its citizens cannot read or write.

Covering almost an entire subcontinent, India is the seventh largest country in the world; nonetheless it is terribly overpopulated. Its 1.2 <u>billion</u> people are second only to China's 1.3 billion, who live in nearly three times the space.

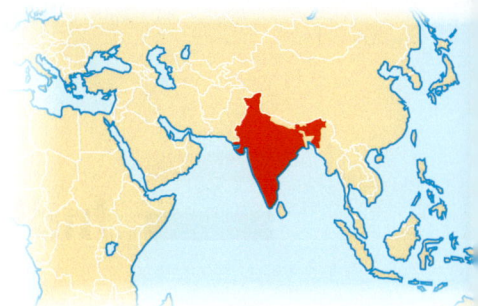

Rich and poor living side by side in Mumbai

5	**a parliamentary system of government** [ˌpɑːləˌmentri ˈsɪstəm]	*ein parlamentarisches Regierungssystem*	N **parliament** [ˈpɑːləmənt] *Parlament* V **govern** [ˈgʌvn] *regieren*
6	**the world's largest democracy** [dɪˈmɒkrəsi]	*der größte demokratische Staat der Welt*	! stress: **de**mocracy [-ˈ---] A **democratic** [ˌdeməˈkrætɪk]
8	**cover** an area	*sich über ein Gebiet erstrecken, ein bestimmtes Gebiet umfassen*	= **spread over an area**
	subcontinent [ˌsʌbˈkɒntɪnənt]	*Subkontinent (= Teil eines Kontinents, der aufgrund seiner Größe und Gestalt eine gewisse Eigenständigkeit hat)*	**continent** [ˈkɒntɪnənt] *Erdteil, Kontinent* A **continental** [ˌkɒntɪˈnentl] *Kontinental..., kontinental*; BE *kontinentaleuropäisch (= Großbritannien und Irland nicht einschließend)*
10	**overpopulated** [ˌəʊvəˈpɒpjuleɪtɪd]	*über(be)völkert*	**densely/heavily populated** ◀▶ **thinly populated** V **populate** [ˈpɒpjuleɪt] *bevölkern* N **population** [ˌpɒpjuˈleɪʃn] *Bevölkerung*

GET THE CONTEXT

■ **India in facts and figures (1)**

Official name	Republic of India		Structure	federal republic: 28 states, 7 union territories
Location	South Asia			
Area	3,287,240 km² (7th in world)		Political system	parliamentary democracy (the world's largest)
Capital	New Delhi			
Population	1.2 bn (2nd in world)		Head of government	Prime Minister
Largest cities	Mumbai/Bombay (19.7 m), Delhi (21.7 m), Kolkata/Calcutta (15.2 m)			
			Head of state	President
Urban/Rural pop.	29% / 71%		Currency	Indian rupee [ruːˈpiː]

2 Colonial past and its consequences

India started to take on its current shape with the arrival of a British presence in the 17th century. As the largest and most profitable colony of the British Empire, India became known
15 during the reign of Queen Victoria (1837–1901) as the 'Jewel in the Crown'. The 'Raj' (Hindi for 'reign'), as the British colonial period was known, brought progress in the form of infrastructure, but the time was also marked by mismanagement as well as food shortages and disease that left millions dead. Resentment
20 against the colonial power grew, and with it the Indian independence movement.

When the British granted India independence in 1947, they divided the former colony into two separate countries, a Muslim Pakistan (which later separated into Pakistan and Bangladesh)
25 and a Hindu India. 'Partition', as the split was known, led to tremendous hardship and sectarian violence, with up to a million deaths. To this day, the two countries are rivals, if not enemies. Both of them maintain huge armies and have developed nuclear weapons out of fear of the other.

'Hindi' – 'Hindu'

N|A **Hindi** ['hɪndi] **1.** Hindi (eine der Amtssprachen Indiens); **2.** Hindi...

N|A **Hindu** ['hɪnduː, ˌhɪn'duː] **1.** Hindu (Anhänger/in des Hinduismus, einer der Hauptreligionen Indiens); **2.** hinduistisch

Collocations with 'colonial'

colonial period/era ['pɪəriəd, 'ɪərə ☆ 'ɪrə, 'erə] Kolonialzeit
colonial past koloniale Vergangenheit
a colonial power eine Kolonialmacht
colonial rule Kolonialherrschaft

CHECKPOINT — *In English, please!*

a *Krankheiten, durch die Millionen von Menschen starben*
b *Indien die Unabhängigkeit gewähren / Indien in die Unabhängigkeit entlassen*
c *die ehemalige Kolonie in zwei verschiedene Staaten aufteilen*
d *riesige Armeen unterhalten*

13 **presence** ['prezns]	*Präsenz, Anwesenheit*	◊ **absence** ['æbsəns] *Abwesenheit* ❗ stress: **presence** ['--] A **present** ['preznt] *anwesend, da, vorhanden*
14 **colony** ['kɒləni]	*Kolonie*	V **colonize** ['kɒlənaɪz] *kolonisieren, besiedeln* A **colonial** [kə'ləʊniəl] *Kolonial..., kolonial* N **colonialism** [kə'ləʊniəlɪzəm] *Kolonialismus*
the British Empire ['empaɪə]	*das Britische Weltreich, das Empire*	**empire** *Reich, Imperium* N **emperor** ['empərə] / **empress** ['emprəs] *Kaiser/in*
15 **the jewel in the crown** ['dʒuːəl, kraʊn]	*das Glanzstück; die Krönung*	**jewel** *Edelstein, Diamant* N|V **crown** 1. *Krone*; 2. *krönen*
16 **the Raj** [rɑːdʒ, rɑːʒ]	*die britische Kolonialherrschaft in Indien (1858–1947); auch: Britisch-Indien*	
17 **infrastructure** ['ɪnfrəstrʌktʃə]	*Infrastruktur*	A **infrastructural** [ˌɪnfrə'strʌktʃərəl] *die Infrastruktur betreffend, infrastrukturell*
21 **independence movement** [ˌɪndɪ'pendəns]	*Unabhängigkeitsbewegung*	A **independent** *unabhängig* ❗ prepositions: **independence from** (Britain) – **independent of/from** ◊ **dependent on**
25 **(the) Partition (of India)** [pɑː'tɪʃn]	*die Aufteilung* (des Kolonial-gebiets in zwei Staaten: Indien und Pakistan)	**partition** *Teilung* (eines Landes) ❗ *Teilung* (allgemein) = **division** [dɪ'vɪʒn] V **part** (sich) *trennen*
26 **sectarian violence** [sekˌteəriən 'vaɪələns]	*religiös motivierte Gewalt*	N **sect** [sekt] *Sekte* A **violent** ['vaɪələnt] *gewalttätig*
29 **nuclear weapons** [ˌnjuːkliə 'wepənz]	*Atomwaffen, Kernwaffen, Nuklearwaffen*	= **atomic weapons** [ə'tɒmɪk] N **nucleus** ['njuːkliəs] *(Atom-, Zell-)Kern*

3 Economic advances

30 Besides being a nuclear power, India is well on its way to becoming an economic superpower. Since independence, the country's industry has expanded to produce a wide range of goods, from toys to aircraft.

The adult literacy rate nationwide increased from 17 per cent in
35 1951 to 74 per cent in 2011 (when the last census was taken); among the nation's youth the rate rose to 82 per cent.

In the urban working world, women have established themselves in every profession.

'economic' – 'economical'

A **economic** [ˌiːkəˈnɒmɪk, ˌekəˈnɒmɪk]
ökonomisch, die Wirtschaft betreffend, Wirtschafts...
economic growth
Wirtschaftswachstum
economic advances *wirtschaftliche Fortschritte, wirtschaftliche Erfolge*
an economic superpower
eine wirtschaftliche Supermacht

A **economical** *wirtschaftlich, sparsam*
an economical car *ein sparsames Auto*

ADV **economically** [ˌiːkəˈnɒmɪkli, ˌekə-]
economically advanced countries

GET THE CONTEXT

■ India in facts and figures (2)

Access to improved water	89%
Access to improved sanitation	33%
Life expectancy	64 years
Infant mortality (to age 1 year)	48 per 1000 live births
Under-5 mortality	66 per 1000
Underweight children under 5	44%

Leading cause of death

• ages 1–4 years	Diarrhoeal diseases (24% of deaths)
• ages 5–14 years	Diarrhoeal diseases (17%)
• ages 15–24 years	Suicide (16%)
Literacy rate	74% (82% for males, 65% for females)
Primary school	83% of primary-aged children enrolled
Mobile phone users	73%
Internet users	11%

30 **a nuclear power**	*eine Nuklearmacht, eine Atommacht*	**nuclear power 1.** *Atommacht;* **2.** *Atomkraft* (= nuclear energy)
32 **expand** [ɪk'spænd]	*sich ausdehnen, expandieren*	N **expansion** [ɪk'spænʃn] *Ausdehnung, Erweiterung*
33 **goods** (pl)	*Güter, Waren*	**goods and services** *Waren und Dienstleistungen*
34 **literacy rate** ['lɪtərəsi]	*Anzahl der Menschen, die lesen und schreiben können; Alphabetisierungsrate*	◊ **illiteracy rate** [ɪ'lɪtərəsi] *Analphabetenrate* A **be literate** ['lɪtərət] *lesen und schreiben können* ! **literary** ['lɪtərəri] *literarisch, Literatur...*
35 **census** ['sensəs]	*(Volks-)Zählung, Zensus*	**carry out / conduct / take a census** *eine Volkszählung durchführen*
■ **access** ['ækses]	*Zugang*	! **ac**cess ['ækses] *Zugang, Zugriff* **ex**cess [ɪk'ses] *Übermaß* A **accessible** [ək'sesəbl] *erreichbar, zugänglich*
■ **sanitation** (no pl) [ˌsænɪ'teɪʃn]	*sanitäre Anlagen, Abwasserentsorgung*	**poor/basic/good/improved/proper sanitation**
■ **life expectancy** [ɪk'spektənsi]	*Lebenserwartung*	V **expect** *erwarten* A **expectant** [ɪk'spektənt] *erwartungsvoll, werdend (Mutter/Vater)*
■ **infant mortality** [ˌɪnfənt mɔ:'tæləti]	*Säuglingssterblichkeit, Kindersterblichkeit*	**infant** ['ɪnfənt] *Säugling, Kleinkind* A **mortal** ['mɔ:tl] *sterblich* ◊ **immortal**
■ **live birth** [laɪv]	*Lebendgeburt*	◊ **stillbirth** *Totgeburt* ! pronunciation: A **live** [laɪv] *lebend, lebendig; live* V **live** [lɪv] *leben, wohnen*
■ **diarrhoea** [ˌdaɪə'rɪə]	*Durchfall*	**diarrhoea** (BE) = **diarrhea** (AE) A **diarrhoeal** [ˌdaɪə'rɪəl] *Durchfall...*

4 A booming job market

With over a billion people and a growing middle class, the
country offers an attractive market. On the other hand, cheap
labour and the fact that many of its people speak English has
made India an ideal location not only for manufacturing, but
also for service-industry jobs, most notably call centres.

The Indian workforce is well trained, and its engineers, especially
in the field of information technology (IT), are sought after all
over the world. Some 20 million Indians, many of whom are
among the best educated in their country, live and work abroad.

At home, millions continue to live in extreme poverty on the
streets or in the slums of Mumbai and other large cities. It will
be a while before they can reap the benefits of their country's
newly found wealth.

'My snake went to work in one of
those call centres.'

Collocations with 'labour' (BE) / 'labor' (AE)
cheap labour *billige Arbeitskräfte*
skilled labour *Facharbeiter/innen*
unskilled labour *ungelernte Arbeitskräfte*
foreign labour *ausländische Arbeitskräfte*
child labour *Kinderarbeit*
slave labour *Sklavenarbeit; Sklaven- arbeiter/innen*
forced labour *Zwangsarbeit; Zwangs- arbeiter/innen*
manual labour ['mænjuəl] *Handarbeit, körperliche Arbeit*

CHECKPOINT — *In English, please!*

a *Indien zu einem idealen Ort für Callcenter machen*
b *im Ausland leben und arbeiten*
c *(auch) weiterhin in extremer Armut leben*
d *die Früchte des neuen Wohlstands ernten*

39 **a growing middle class** [ˌmɪdl ˈklɑːs]	*eine wachsende Mittelschicht*	V **grow, grew, grown** *wachsen, zunehmen* N **growth** *Wachstum, Anwachsen, Zunahme* **the working class** *die Arbeiterklasse* **the upper class** *die Oberschicht*
42 **manufacturing** [ˌmænjuˈfæktʃərɪŋ]	*Herstellung, Produktion*	V **manufacture** [ˌmænjuˈfæktʃə] *herstellen, produzieren* N **manufacturer** *Hersteller* (von Gerät usw.)
43 **service-industry job**	*Beruf im Dienstleistungsgewerbe*	= **a job in an industry that provides a service rather than a product**
call centre	*Callcenter, Telefonzentrale*	**centre** (BE) = **center** (AE)
44 **workforce** [ˈwɜːkfɔːs] (+ sing or pl verb)	*Arbeitskräfte, Belegschaft*	= **labour force** **force** *Truppe*
45 **information technology (IT)** [tekˈnɒlədʒi]	*Informationstechnologie (IT)*	V **inform** *informieren* ! pronunciation: **technology** [tekˈnɒlədʒi] *Technik (= Fertigkeit, Methode, Arbeitstechnik)* = **technique** [tekˈniːk]
48 **poverty** [ˈpɒvəti]	*Armut*	◊ **wealth** [welθ] *Reichtum, Vermögen* **live at/below the poverty line** *an/unter der Armutsgrenze leben* A **poor** *arm*
49 **slum** [slʌm]	*Slum, Elendsviertel*	**city/urban slums** *Armenviertel der Großstädte, städtische Elendsviertel* **slum dweller** *Slumbewohner/in* **live in slum conditions** *in elenden Verhältnissen leben*

broaden
Marshall
Plan
restoration
exchange

anti-Americanism

democracy

financial

aid

military.

influence

curb

engineering

European

diplomatic

permanent
seat

role

world

cultural

Old World

NATO

UN Security
Council

Recovery

peace

sovereignty

respect

take on

war

prowess

Holocaust

references

freedom

restore

spread of
terrorism

obligation

economic

powerhouse

sphere of
influence

deployment

gratitude

totalitarianism

admiration

reunification

reconstruction

New

descent

World

image

Germany in the World

1 The many faces of Germany

Germany means different things to different people. To some it is an economic powerhouse that produces and exports high-quality, expensive goods.

To others it is the place where democracy and freedom have twice conquered totalitarianism in the last century.

And for many it is primarily the country responsible for two world wars and the Holocaust.

ITALIAN DESIGN, GERMAN ENGINEERING...

...ALL YOU'D EXPECT IN A BRITISH CAR!

CARS

©Flantoons

CHECKPOINT — *In English, please!*

a *für jeden etwas anderes bedeuten*
b *hochwertige Güter herstellen*
c *den Totalitarismus besiegen / den Totalitarismus überwinden*

German 'Weltkrieg'

world war *Weltkrieg*
World War One = World War I
  = the First World War
  der Erste Weltkrieg (1914–1918)
World War Two = World War II
  = the Second World War
  der Zweite Weltkrieg (1939–1945)
the global war on terror *der weltweite/ globale Krieg gegen den Terror*

2 **economic powerhouse** [ˌiːkəˈnɒmɪk, ˌekəˈnɒmɪk]	*Wirtschaftsmacht, Wirtschafts-motor, Konjunkturlokomotive*	N **economy** [ɪˈkɒnəmi] *Wirtschaft* N **economics** [ˌiːkəˈnɒmɪks] *Wirtschaftswissen-schaften*
4 **democracy** [dɪˈmɒkrəsi]	*Demokratie*	! stress: **democracy** [-´---] A **democratic** [ˌdeməˈkrætɪk] *demokratisch* N **democrat** [ˈdeməkræt] *Demokrat/in*
freedom [ˈfriːdəm]	*Freiheit*	= **liberty** ! *Frieden* = **peace**
5 **totalitarianism** [təʊˌtæləˈteəriənɪzəm]	*Totalitarismus*	A **totalitarian** *totalitär (= mit diktatorischen Methoden jegliche Demokratie unterdrückend)*
7 **the Holocaust** [ˈhɒləkɔːst]	*der Holocaust; der Völkermord (besonders an den Juden wäh-rend des Nationalsozialismus)*	**holocaust** *Inferno* **a nuclear holocaust** *ein Atominferno*

GET THE CONTEXT

Landmarks in German history

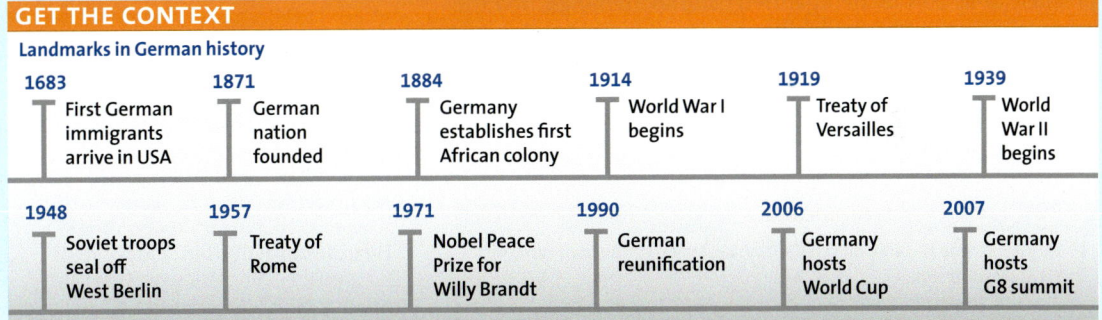

1683	1871	1884	1914	1919	1939
First German immigrants arrive in USA	German nation founded	Germany establishes first African colony	World War I begins	Treaty of Versailles	World War II begins

1948	1957	1971	1990	2006	2007
Soviet troops seal off West Berlin	Treaty of Rome	Nobel Peace Prize for Willy Brandt	German reunification	Germany hosts World Cup	Germany hosts G8 summit

2 British images of Germany

The association of Germany with the Second World War and little else is quite strong in Britain. Sport competitions between
10 UK and German teams are often accompanied by military references (e.g. 'Blitz the Fritz') in the popular press. And nearly every Briton has tales to tell of 'towel wars' with early-rising Germans who, at holiday hotels, reserve sunbeds with their towels before breakfast.

15 But the British image of Germany also has room for admiration. There is great respect in the UK for German engineering prowess. And young people, especially those who have visited Germany privately or as part of an organized cultural exchange, find the country quite trendy, most notably the capital city of Berlin with
20 its subcultures and fashion and techno scenes.

'Bloody typical.'
(„Wieder mal echt typisch!")

English (offensive) terms sometimes used for Germans

the Fritz (slang) – used especially during World Wars I and II
Jerry, pl Jerries (taboo, BE, slang) – used especially during World Wars I and II
Hun, pl Huns or the Hun (infml) – used especially during World Wars I and II
Kraut, pl Krauts (taboo, slang)

CHECKPOINT — *In English, please!*

a *die gedankliche Verbindung von Deutschland mit dem Zweiten Weltkrieg*
b *die Boulevardpresse*
c *das britische Deutschlandbild*

10 **military references** [ˌmɪlətri ☆ ˌmɪləteri 'refrənsɪz]	*militärische Hinweise,* *militärische Bezüge*	N **the military** *das Militär* **make (a) reference to** sth. *etw. erwähnen, auf etw.* *Bezug nehmen* V **refer to** sth. **(-rr-)** [rɪ'fɜː] *sich auf etw. beziehen,* *auf etw. verweisen*
15 **image of Germany** ['ɪmɪdʒ]	*Deutschlandbild;* *Vorstellung von Deutschland*	**image 1.** *Vorstellung, Idee;* **2.** *Image, öffentliches* *Ansehen;* **3.** *Abbild;* **4.** *bildlicher Ausdruck, Metapher* (cf. p. 167) V **imagine** [ɪ'mædʒɪn] *sich vorstellen*
admiration [ˌædmə'reɪʃn]	*Bewunderung*	V **admire** [əd'maɪə] *bewundern* N **admirer** *Bewunderer/-in, Verehrer/in* A **admirable** ['ædmərəbl] *bewundernswert*
16 **respect** [rɪ'spekt]	*Achtung, Respekt*	◊ **disrespect** [ˌdɪsrɪ'spekt] *Respektlosigkeit* **have (no) respect for** sth./sb. *(keinen) Respekt vor* *etw./jdm. haben* V **respect** *achten, respektieren* A **respectful** *respektvoll* A **respectable** [rɪ'spektəbl] *seriös, angesehen*
engineering prowess (fml) [ˌendʒɪˌnɪərɪŋ 'praʊəs]	*technisches Können, Ingenieurs-* *kunst*	**engineering** *Ingenieurwesen, Technik und Konstruk-* *tion* **mechanical engineering** *Maschinenbau* N **engineer** [ˌendʒɪ'nɪə] *Ingenieur/in, Techniker/in*
18 **a cultural exchange** [ˌkʌltʃərəl_ɪks'tʃeɪndʒ]	*ein kultureller Austausch*	N **culture** ['kʌltʃə] *Kultur* **go on an exchange** *an einem Austausch(programm)* *teilnehmen* V **exchange** *austauschen*

3 Germany and the USA

Germany's relationship with America began even before the USA was founded, when Germans were among the earliest settlers in the New World. Americans of German descent are proud of their heritage and practise many traditions from the Old World,
25 although their knowledge of modern Germany is often limited, ending with World War II.

After the war the US government was more interested in broadening its sphere of influence than in punishing its former enemy. The European Recovery Program, also known as the
30 Marshall Plan, included some $1.4 billion in financial aid to Germany for reconstruction. At the same time, the USA – like the other western Allies, the UK and France, – maintained a large number of troops in the Federal Republic of Germany and in the western sectors of Berlin.

35 On the whole, Americans expected more gratitude for their financial and military aid to Germany. Instead, many Germans were highly critical of, for example, America's war in Vietnam or the deployment of American missiles in their country. Anti-Americanism was strong in Germany during the final
40 decades of the 20th century and into the 21st.

Collocations with 'aid' [eɪd]
financial aid [faɪˈnænʃl] *finanzielle Hilfe, finanzielle Unterstützung*
economic aid *Wirtschaftshilfe*
military aid *Militärhilfe*
medical aid *medizinische Hilfe*
humanitarian aid *humanitäre Hilfe*
emergency aid [iˈmɜːdʒənsi] *Nothilfe, Soforthilfe, Katastrophenhilfe*
foreign aid [ˈfɒrɪn] *Entwicklungshilfe*
first aid *Erste Hilfe*

appeal/call for aid *um Hilfe bitten*
give/provide aid *Hilfe leisten/gewähren*
receive aid *Hilfe erhalten*
accept aid *Hilfe annehmen*
depend/rely on aid *auf Hilfe angewiesen sein, sich auf Hilfe verlassen*

CHECKPOINT *In English, please!*

a *stolz auf sein Erbe sein*
b *begrenzte Kenntnisse des modernen Deutschlands haben*
c *an der Ausdehnung des eigenen Machtbereichs interessiert sein*
d *dem Krieg der Amerikaner in Vietnam höchst kritisch gegenüberstehen*

23 **the New World**	*die Neue Welt*	= **North, Central and South America**
Americans of German descent [dɪˈsent]	*Amerikaner/innen deutscher Abstammung/Herkunft*	= **Americans of German ancestry/origin** [ˈɒrɪdʒɪn] v **be descended from** [dɪˈsendɪd] *abstammen von* N **descendant** [dɪˈsendənt] *Nachkomme* ! spelling and pronunciation: de**scent** [dɪˈsent] *Abstammung* de**cent** [ˈdiːsnt] *anständig*
24 **the Old World**	*die Alte Welt*	= **Europe, Asia and Africa**
28 **broaden** one's **sphere** [sfɪə] **of influence**	*seinen Einflussbereich/ Machtbereich erweitern*	A **broad** [brɔːd] *weit, ausgedehnt* v **influence** *beeinflussen*
31 **reconstruction** [ˌriːkənˈstrʌkʃn]	*Wiederaufbau*	v **reconstruct** *wiederaufbauen*
35 **gratitude** [ˈgrætɪtjuːd]	*Dankbarkeit*	◊ **ingratitude** *Undankbarkeit* A **(un)grateful** *(un)dankbar*
38 **deployment** [dɪˈplɔɪmənt]	*Aufstellung, Stationierung* (von Raketen, Truppen)	v **deploy** (Raketen) *aufstellen*, (Truppen) *stationieren*
39 **anti-Americanism** [ˌænti_əˈmerɪkənɪzəm]	*Antiamerikanismus; eine antiamerikanische Haltung*	◊ **pro-Americanism**

GET THE CONTEXT

■ **the European Recovery Program (ERP)** [rɪˈkʌvəri] *das europäische Wiederaufbauprogramm*
The European Recovery Program, also known as **the Marshall Plan**, was devised in 1947 by the US State Department to rebuild and strengthen the economic foundations of Western European countries after World War II. It was in operation from 1948–1952 with a budget of over $13 billion in economic and technical assistance.
The Marshall Plan was named after then US Secretary of State George Marshall.

4 German diplomacy

With <u>Reunification</u> and the <u>restoration</u> of full sovereignty, Germany began to take on a new, expanded role in the world. Suddenly Germany, as a member of <u>the North Atlantic Treaty Organization (NATO)</u>, had military obligations to help keep or
₄₅ <u>restore</u> the peace in far-flung countries around the globe, to stop piracy or to curb the spread of terrorism.

Germany's <u>diplomatic influence</u> has increased as well. No important international conference on the economy or the environment is conceivable without German input, and there is
₅₀ even talk of giving Germany a permanent seat on <u>the United Nations Security Council</u>.

The fall of the Berlin Wall paved the way to Reunification on 3 October 1990.

The pronunciation of 're-'			
reunify	[riː]	*reunification*	[riː]
reconstruct	[riː]	*reconstruction*	[riː]
restore	[rɪ] But:	*restoration*	[re]
refer	[rɪ] But:	*reference*	[re]
reserve	[rɪ] But:	*reservation*	[re]

Word family 'diplomat'

N **diplomat** ['dɪpləmæt] *Diplomat/in*
A **diplomatic** [ˌdɪplə'mætɪk] *diplomatisch*
  diplomatic influence
  diplomatic relations
N **diplomacy** [dɪ'pləʊməsi] *Diplomatie*

CHECKPOINT ◁ *In English, please!*

a *Mitglied (in) der Nato sein*
b *den Frieden erhalten / bewahren*
c *eine internationale Konferenz zur Umwelt*
d *Deutschland einen ständigen Sitz im UN-Sicherheitsrat geben*

41 **reunification** [ˌriːjuːnɪfɪˈkeɪʃn]	*Wiedervereinigung*	V **reunify** [ˌriːˈjuːnɪfaɪ] *wiedervereinigen*
the restoration of full sovereignty [ˌrestəˈreɪʃn, ˈsɒvrənti] (fml)	*die Herstellung voller, uneingeschränkter Souveränität/ Eigenstaatlichkeit*	V **restore** [rɪˈstɔː] *wiederherstellen* N|A **sovereign** (fml) **1.** *Herrscher/in*; **2.** *souverän (Staat)* **!** pronunciation: **sovereign** [ˈsɒvrɪn ☆ ˈsɑːvrən]
42 **take on a new, expanded role** [ɪkˈspændɪd]	*eine neue, erweiterte Rolle/ Funktion übernehmen*	N **expansion** [ɪkˈspænʃn] *Ausdehnung, Erweiterung* **!** homophones: **role – roll** *Rolle (aus Papier usw.)*
44 **a military obligation** [ˌɒblɪˈɡeɪʃn]	*eine militärische Verpflichtung*	**take on / have / fulfil an obligation** A **obligatory** [əˈblɪɡətri ☆ əˈblɪɡətɔːri] *verpflichtend*
45 **restore the peace** [rɪˈstɔː]	*den Frieden wiederherstellen*	**!** homophones: **peace – piece** [piːs] *Stück*
46 **curb the spread of terrorism** [kɜːb, spred, ˈterərɪzəm]	*die Ausbreitung des Terrorismus eindämmen*	V **spread** [spred]**, spread, spread** *(sich) ausbreiten* N **terror** [ˈterə] *Terror, panische Angst* N **terrorist** [ˈterərɪst] *Terrorist/in; Terror...*
50 **a permanent seat** [ˈpɜːmənənt]	*ein ständiger Sitz* (in einem Gremium), *ein permanenter Sitz*	◀▶ **a non-permanent seat** **!** stress: **permanent** [ˈ---]

■ <u>**NATO**</u> [ˈneɪtəʊ] **(= <u>the North Atlantic Treaty Organization</u>)** *die NATO (= die Nordatlantische Vertragsorganisation)*
an alliance of 28 North American and European countries committed to safeguarding the freedom and security of its member countries by political and military means
! No article: **our allies in Nato** ... *in der Nato*

■ <u>**the United Nations Security Council**</u> [sɪˈkjʊərəti ˌkaʊnsl]
der Sicherheitsrat der Vereinten Nationen, der UN-Sicherheitsrat
a principal organ of the United Nations, made up of 15 nations. Five of these nations – China, France, Russia, the UK and the USA – are permanent members; the other ten are elected for two-year terms. The Security Council has the power to decide on resolutions concerning peacekeeping operations, international sanctions and the authorization of military action. The permanent members have the right to veto planned resolutions.

Global Perspectives

1 Advantages of globalization

2 Victims of globalization

3 Support for 'ethical manufacturing'

4 Increasing dependency on the global economy

5 Efforts to improve international relations

1 Advantages of globalization

The word 'globalization' usually refers to the breaking down of trade barriers between nations.

For supporters of globalization, the deregulation of trade and the elimination of national protectionism are positive things:
5 without trade barriers, goods can pass freely from one part of the world to another. In this way, people in developing countries gain access to world markets.

At the same time, the competition between companies allows the consumers in developed countries to buy goods at lower
10 prices. The market forces of supply and demand regulate prices.

Word family 'globe'

N **globe** [gləʊb] *Globus, Welt(kugel)*
A **global** ['gləʊbl] *weltweit, global*
ADV **globally** *weltweit, global, allgemein*
V **globalize** (BE also: **globalise**)
   ['gləʊbəlaɪz] *globalisieren*
N **globalization** (BE also: **globalisation**)
   [ˌgləʊbəlaɪˈzeɪʃn ☆ ˌgləʊbələˈzeɪʃn]
   Globalisierung

Word family 'compete'

V **compete** [kəmˈpiːt] *konkurrieren*
N **competition** [ˌkɒmpəˈtɪʃn] *Konkurrenz, Wettbewerb; Konkurrenzfirmen, Rivalen, Gegner*
A **competitive** [kəmˈpetətɪv] *konkurrierend, Wettbewerbs...; konkurrenzfähig*
N **competitiveness** [kəmˈpetətɪvnəs] *Wettbewerbsfähigkeit*
N **competitor** [kəmˈpetɪtə] *Konkurrent/in, Wettbewerber/in*

CHECKPOINT — *In English, please!*

a *die Beseitigung von nationalem Protektionismus*
b *ungehindert von einem Teil der Welt in einen anderen gelangen*
c *Zugang zu den Weltmärkten erhalten*
d *Waren zu niedrigeren Preisen kaufen*

1 **break down trade barriers** ['bæriəz]**, broke, broken**	*Handelsbarrieren/Handels-schranken abbauen*	= **reduce/remove trade barriers** ◊ **erect trade barriers** *Handelsschranken errichten*
3 **supporter of globalization** [sə'pɔːtə]	*Globalisierungsbefürworter/in*	V|N **support** 1. *unterstützen;* 2. *Unterstützung* A **supportive** [sə'pɔːtɪv] *(unter)stützend*
deregulation [ˌdiːˌregjuˈleɪʃn]	*Deregulierung; Marktöffnung*	◊ **regulation** *Regelung, Regulierung; Vorschrift* V **deregulate** [ˌdiːˈregjuleɪt] *deregulieren, freigeben*
4 **protectionism** [prəˈtekʃənɪzm]	*Protektionismus (= Begünsti-gung der inländischen Pro-duktion, z.B. durch Schutzzölle)*	V **protect** *(be)schützen* N **protection** [prəˈtekʃn] *Schutz* A **protectionist** [prəˈtekʃənɪst] *protektionistisch*
5 **goods** (pl)	*Güter, Waren*	**goods and services** *Waren und Dienstleistungen*
6 **developing country** [dɪˈveləpɪŋ]	*Entwicklungsland*	V **develop** *(sich) entwickeln* N **development** [dɪˈveləpmənt] *Entwicklung*
7 **access to world markets** ['ækses]	*Zugang zu (den) Weltmärkten*	! **ac**cess ['**æk**ses] *Zugang, Zugriff* **ex**cess [**ɪk**'ses] *Übermaß* A **accessible** [əkˈsesəbl] *erreichbar, zugänglich*
9 **consumer** [kənˈsjuːmə]	*Konsument/in, Verbraucher/in*	V **consume** [kənˈsjuːm] *verbrauchen, konsumieren* N **consumption** [kənˈsʌmpʃən] *Verbrauch, Konsum*
developed country [dɪˈveləpt]	*Industrieland, Industriestaat, wirtschaftsstarker Staat*	= **industrialized country / industrial nation** ◊ **developing country**
10 **market forces**	*Marktkräfte, die Kräfte des freien Marktes*	**market economy** [ɪˈkɒnəmi] *(freie) Marktwirtschaft*
supply and demand [səˈplaɪ, dɪˈmɑːnd]	*Angebot und Nachfrage*	**the law of supply and demand** *das Gesetz von Angebot und Nachfrage*
regulate sth. ['regjuleɪt]	*etw. regulieren, etw. steuern*	= **control** sth.

2 Victims of globalization

To globalization critics, free trade comes at the expense of workers in developing countries. They work long hours, often in unsafe or unhealthy conditions in so-called sweatshops, where they barely earn a subsistence wage and do not enjoy
15 job security. These factories often use child labour. Trade unions try to organize workers and improve working conditions, but these attempts are often met with violence.

At the same time, skilled and unskilled workers in the developed world feel that they too are victims of global-
20 ization. Their employers compare production costs of plants at home and abroad and conclude that domestic production is too costly. Jobs are then outsourced to a developing country with a huge labour force. These employees are willing to work for considerably lower wages.

Word family 'skill'

N **skill** *Fertigkeit, berufliche Qualifikation*
A **skilful** (BE) / **skillful** (AE) *geschickt*
A **skilled** *ausgebildet, qualifiziert*
   skilled worker *Facharbeiter/in*
A **unskilled** *ungelernt* (Arbeiter, Arbeit)
   unskilled worker *Hilfsarbeiter/in*

Word family 'employ'

V **employ** [ɪmˈplɔɪ] *anstellen, beschäftigen*
A **employable** [ɪmˈplɔɪəbl] *vermittelbar, anstellbar, im Beruf einsetzbar*
N **employer** [ɪmˈplɔɪə] *Arbeitgeber/in, Unternehmer/in*
N **employee** [ɪmˈplɔɪiː] *Arbeitnehmer/in, Angestellte(r), Mitarbeiter/in*
N **employment** [ɪmˈplɔɪmənt] *Beschäftigung, Arbeit, Anstellung*
N **unemployment** *Arbeitslosigkeit*
A **unemployed** *arbeitslos*

German 'Lohn'

pay *allgemeine Bezeichnung für die Bezahlung geleisteter Arbeit*
wage [weɪdʒ], also **wages** (pl) *(Tages-, Wochen-)Lohn*
salary *(monatlich überwiesenes) Gehalt*

CHECKPOINT — *In English, please!*

a *auf Kosten der Arbeiter gehen*
b *lange arbeiten / Überstunden machen*
c *im In- und Ausland*
d *bereit sein, für deutlich weniger Lohn zu arbeiten*

11 **globalization critic** ['krɪtɪk]	*Globalisierungskritiker/in*	**!** **critic** *Kritiker/in* – **criticism** ['krɪtɪsɪzəm] *Kritik* **v** **criticize** ['krɪtɪsaɪz] *kritisieren* **a** **critical** ['krɪtɪkl] *kritisch*
13 **unsafe/unhealthy conditions** [ˌʌn'helθi kən'dɪʃnz]	*unsichere/ungesunde Verhält-nisse/Bedingungen*	◆ **safe/healthy conditions**
sweatshop ['swetʃɒp]	*Ausbeuterbetrieb*	**!** pronunciation: **sweat** [swet] *Schweiß*
14 **earn a subsistence wage** [ɜːn, səb'sɪstəns]	*einen Lohn verdienen, der nur den Lebensunterhalt deckt*	**!** *verdienen* = 1. **earn** (money); 2. **deserve** (what you should get) [dɪ'zɜːv]
15 **job security** [sɪ'kjʊərəti]	*Arbeitsplatzsicherheit, Sicherheit vor Entlassung*	◆ **job insecurity** *Arbeitsplatzunsicherheit* **enjoy/have job security**
child labour ['leɪbə]	*Kinderarbeit*	**labour** (BE) = **labor** (AE)
trade union [ˌtreɪd 'juːniən]	*Gewerkschaft*	**trade union** (BE) = **labor union** (AE)
16 **organize workers** ['ɔːgənaɪz]	*(die) Arbeiter/Arbeitnehmer organisieren*	**n** **workers' organization** [ˌɔːgənaɪ'zeɪʃn] *Arbeit-nehmerorganisation*
improve working conditions [ɪm'pruːv]	*(die) Arbeitsbedingungen verbessern*	**improve** 1. *etw. verbessern;* 2. *sich verbessern* **n** **improvement** *Verbesserung*
20 **production costs** [prə'dʌkʃn kɒsts]	*Produktionskosten, Herstellungs-kosten*	**v** **produce** [prə'djuːs] *produzieren, herstellen*
plant [plɑːnt]	*Niederlassung; Werksanlage*	**plant** 1. *Pflanze;* 2. *Fabrik, Betrieb*
21 **domestic production** [də'mestɪk]	*(die) Inlandsproduktion*	◆ **overseas production / production abroad**
22 **outsource** sth. ['aʊtsɔːs]	*etw. ausgliedern; etw. nach außen verlagern*	**n** **outsourcing** ◆ **insourcing / bringing it in-house**
23 **labour force** (+ sing or pl verb)	*Arbeitskräfte, erwerbstätige Bevölkerung; Belegschaft*	= **workforce** **force** *Truppe*

3 Support for 'ethical manufacturing'

25 It is becoming increasingly possible for consumers to <u>affect</u> the way workers are treated in developing countries.

Under threat of boycotts by concerned consumers, some multinational companies, especially in the textile industry, have committed themselves to 'ethical manufacturing'. A brand's
30 image is important to the company, so it will do its best to avoid bad press. Therefore some companies encourage the countries from which they import their goods to protect the rights of their workers.

Many globalization opponents avoid big brands altogether
35 and buy 'fair trade' products made by workers who receive a fair wage and work in a safe and healthy workplace.

CHECKPOINT — *In English, please!*

a *Einfluss darauf nehmen, wie Arbeiter behandelt werden*
b *sich zur „ethischen Produktion" verpflichten*
c *alles tun, um negative Medienberichte zu vermeiden*
d *ganz auf Waren großer Markenkonzerne verzichten*

The international FAIRTRADE Mark

27 **boycott** ['bɔɪkɒt]	*Boykott, bewusstes Meiden*	**!** stress: <u>**boy**</u>cott ['--] **call for / impose / organize a boycott (of/on** sth.) v **boycott** *boykottieren*
28 **a multinational company** [ˌmʌltiˌnæʃnəl 'kʌmpəni]	*ein multinationaler Konzern (= ein in vielen Staaten vertretener Konzern)*	= **a global player** ◀▶ **a national company** **multi...** (prefix) = **more than one; many**
29 **brand**	*(Handels-)Marke; Sorte*	**brand name** = **trade name** *Markenname* **!** *Brand* = **fire**
30 **image** ['ɪmɪdʒ]	*Image; Persönlichkeitsbild*	**improve a company's (public) image**
31 **bad press**	*(eine) schlechte Presse, negative Publicity*	◀▶ **good press** **have / get / be given (a) bad press**
32 **import goods** [ɪm'pɔːt]	*Güter importieren, Güter einführen*	◀▶ **export goods** [ɪk'spɔːt] **!** stress: v **im**<u>**port**</u>/**ex**<u>**port**</u> [-'-] **goods** N the <u>**im**</u>port/<u>**ex**</u>port ['-- /'eks-] **of goods**
	protect the rights of workers [prə'tekt]	*die Rechte der Arbeiter/innen schützen, Arbeitnehmerrechte schützen*	N **protection** *Schutz* **!** *Recht* = **1. right** *Anspruch, Berechtigung;* **2. law** *Gesamtheit der Gesetze, Rechtssystem*
34 **globalization opponent** [ə'pəʊnənt]	*Globalisierungsgegner/in*	= **globalization critic / anti-globalization activist** ◀▶ **supporter of globalization** v **oppose** sth. (Plan, Idee usw.) *ablehnen*
36 **workplace**	*Arbeitsplatz*	**!** *Arbeitsplatz* = **1. workplace** *Arbeitsstätte* **in the workplace** *am Arbeitsplatz* **2. job** *Stelle, Stellung* **job creation** *die Schaffung von Arbeitsplätzen*

4 Increasing dependency on the global economy

One major result of globalization is that – figuratively speaking – the world is getting smaller. Individual countries are more dependent on the global economy than ever before.

40 Just how interdependent the world is became evident in the financial crisis which began in 2008, when bank failures and the bankrupting of entire industries were only prevented by government intervention.

International trade is regulated by the World Trade Organization 45 (WTO), which encourages free trade. WTO summit meetings as well as those of other economic institutions such as the Group of Eight (G8, eight industrialized countries from the northern hemisphere) are targets for lobbying and protests.

CHECKPOINT — *In English, please!*

a *eine der wesentlichen Folgen der Globalisierung sein*
b *mehr denn je von der Weltwirtschaft abhängig sein*
c *den internationalen Handel regulieren*
d *den freien Handel fördern*

Collocations with 'global'

the global economy *die Weltwirtschaft*
the global market *der Weltmarkt*
the global village *das globale Dorf, das Weltdorf (= die durch das Internet zusammengewachsene moderne Welt)*
a global player *ein Weltkonzern, ein Global Player*
global trading *der weltweite Handel*
global warming *die Erderwärmung, die globale Erwärmung*
Global Positioning System (GPS) *satellitengestütztes, weltweites Navigationssystem*

'economic' – 'economical'

A **economic** [ˌiːkəˈnɒmɪk, ˌekəˈnɒmɪk] *ökonomisch, die Wirtschaft betreffend, Wirtschafts...*
economic institutions *Wirtschaftsinstitutionen*
economic growth *Wirtschaftswachstum*

A **economical** *wirtschaftlich, sparsam*
an economical car *ein sparsames Auto*

ADV **economically** [ˌiːkəˈnɒmɪkli, ˌekə-]
economically advanced countries

41	**financial crisis**, pl **crises** [faɪˌnænʃl ˈkraɪsɪz, ˈkraɪsiːz]	*Finanzkrise*	N|V **finance** [ˈfaɪnæns, faɪˈnæns] **1.** *Finanz(en)*; **2.** *finanzieren*
	bank failure [ˈfeɪljə]	*Bankenpleite, -zusammenbruch*	V **fail** *versagen, scheitern*
42	**bankrupt** sb./sth. [ˈbæŋkrʌpt]	*jdn./etw. in den Ruin treiben / finanziell ruinieren*	A **bankrupt: go bankrupt** *Bankrott machen* N **bankruptcy** [ˈbæŋkrʌptsi] *Bankrott, Konkurs*
43	**government intervention** [ˌɪntəˈvenʃn]	*Eingriff der Regierung, staatliche Intervention*	V **intervene** [ˌɪntəˈviːn] *eingreifen, intervenieren*
45	**summit meeting** [ˈsʌmɪt]	*Gipfeltreffen*	= **summit conference** [ˈkɒnfərəns]
47	**industrialized country** [ɪnˈdʌstriəlaɪzd]	*Industrieland, Industriestaat*	= **industrial(ized) nation / developed country** N **industrialization** *Industrialisierung*
48	**lobby** sb.	*(Abgeordnete) beeinflussen*	N **lobby 1.** *Wandelhalle im Parlament, in der die Abgeordneten mit Wählern und Interessengruppen zusammentreffen;* **2.** *Interessengruppe, -verband*

GET THE CONTEXT

■ **the World Trade Organization (WTO)**
die Welthandelsorganisation (WTO)
an international organization consisting of 153 members. It was set up in 1995 and controls and deals with global rules of trade between nations. In addition to the Ministerial Conference in Geneva, Switzerland, which makes the top decisions, there are also a number of working groups and committees like the Goods Council and the Services Council. The WTO has a dispute settlement role and may authorize retaliation *(Strafmaßnahmen)* against countries who violate the rules.

■ **the Group of Eight (G8)** *die Gruppe der Acht (G8)*
an important international forum made up of the eight economically most powerful countries (Canada, France, Germany, Italy, Japan, Russia, the UK and the USA). Founded in 1975 as the G6 (Canada joined a year later, Russia in 1998), the group has set itself the task of trying to solve world problems such as poverty. Its meetings, attended by the heads of the member countries as well as the head of the European Union, are often controversial.

5 Efforts to improve international relations

Besides the organizations that try to regulate the world's
economy, there are international bodies that look after other
aspects of international relations.

The United Nations (UN), for example, deals with health issues,
the problems of refugees and, of course, national and
international conflicts through its peacekeeping missions.
Elsewhere in the world, the European Union, the Commonwealth
and others work to provide security, peace and stability.

Most relief efforts in impoverished countries or disaster areas
are carried out, however, by so-called 'non-governmental organizations' (NGOs) such as Médecins Sans Frontières or Oxfam.
Although they receive some government funding, these
organizations rely largely on donations and volunteer work.

UN peacekeepers

CHECKPOINT — *In English, please!*

a *sich mit Gesundheitsfragen befassen*
b *Sicherheit schaffen / für Sicherheit sorgen*
c *Hilfsmaßnahmen durchführen*
d *weitgehend von Spenden abhängig sein*

51	**international relations** [ɪrˈleɪʃnz]	internationale Beziehungen, Auslandsbeziehungen	**establish / break off diplomatic relations** diplomatische Beziehungen aufnehmen/abbrechen
53	**refugee** [ˌrefjuˈdʒiː]	Flüchtling	N **refuge** [ˈrefjuːdʒ] Zuflucht, Schutz
54	**conflict** [ˈkɒnflɪkt]	Konflikt, Auseinandersetzung	! stress: **conflict** [ˈ--]
57	**relief effort** [rɪˈliːf ˌefət]	Hilfsmaßnahme, Hilfseinsatz	**relief organization** Hilfsorganisation
	an impoverished country [ɪmˈpɒvərɪʃt]	ein verarmtes Land, ein armes Land	= **a poor country** N **poverty** [ˈpɒvəti] Armut
	disaster area [dɪˈzɑːstər ˌeəriə]	Katastrophengebiet	! spelling: **di**saster De**saster, Unglück** A **disastrous** [dɪˈzɑːstrəs] katastrophal
60	**government funding** [ˈfʌndɪŋ]	staatliche Finanzierung	N|v **fund 1.** Fonds, Geldmittel (= **funds**); **2.** finanzieren
61	**donation** [dəʊˈneɪʃn]	Spende	v **donate** spenden – ! **spend** (Geld) ausgeben
	volunteer work [ˌvɒlənˈtɪə]	ehrenamtliche Arbeit	N|v **volunteer 1.** Freiwillige(r); **2.** sich freiwillig melden A **voluntary** [ˈvɒləntri] freiwillig, ehrenamtlich

GET THE CONTEXT

■ **the United Nations (UN)** die Vereinten Nationen
an international organization founded in 1945 by
51 countries intending international peace and
security. Today the organization with its 193 member
states works in a wide range of areas, from environment and refugee protection, disaster relief and economic and
social development to promoting democracy and human rights for
a safe world in the future.

! **UN + singular verb: The United Nations** _deals_ **with …**

■ **non-governmental organizations (NGOs)**
Nichtregierungsorganisationen
private organizations that are officially recognized by
governments, but are set up and managed independently
of them and therefore function without government
status. Although NGOs may be funded by the state, governments have no influence upon how they are run. They
usually have a social aim, e.g. community development,
provision of social services or environmental protection.

do business

retirement

corporate

model

wages

home office

relocate ladder

reduce

in-service professional

multinational costs

training

qualified part-time

work remotely

workplace highly employment

company competitive

hire and fire

reorientation

soft skills skilled manufacturing

emerging industrialized

access service

outsourcing industry

markets

country

to work sector

work from home

rationalization maximize

productivity

invest

low-skilled temporary

unemployment

raise flexitime

promote job employment

profits

rate low-paid

nomad worker

security nine to five

meet automation

workforce

challenges meet demands

office cubicle

The World of Work and Business

1 Maximizing economic growth

With the rise of emerging markets, especially the BRIC countries (Brazil, Russia, India, China), the centre of economic power has been shifting towards the Asian-Pacific region.

5 In order to remain competitive, the industrial nations have to raise the productivity of their economies in a process of automation and rationalization while at the same time investing in research and development to encourage innovation. To reduce costs and to maximize profits, multinational companies often 10 relocate facilities to other countries (= outsourcing) to profit from lower wages and less restrictive laws (on environmental issues, total working hours per day, etc.).

'We're almost fully automated now.'

Word family 'compete'

V **compete** [kəm'piːt] *konkurrieren*
N **competition** [ˌkɒmpə'tɪʃn] *Konkurrenz, Wettbewerb; Konkurrenzfirmen, Rivalen, Gegner*
A **competitive** [kəm'petətɪv] *konkurrenzfähig; konkurrierend, Wettbewerbs...*
N **competitiveness** [kəm'petətɪvnəs] *Wettbewerbsfähigkeit*
N **competitor** [kəm'petətə] *Konkurrent / in, Wettbewerber / in*

1 **emerging markets** [i'mɜːdʒɪŋ]	*Schwellenländer, Wachstums-märkte*	= **emergent markets** v **emerge** *auftauchen, aufkommen, hervortreten*
6 **raise the productivity** [reɪz, ˌprɒdʌk'tɪvəti]	*die Produktivität steigern*	= **increase the productivity** ◊ **lower the productivity** A **productive** [prə'dʌktɪv] *produktiv* ❗ **raise** sth. *etw. anheben, erhöhen* – **rise** *(an)steigen*
7 **automation** [ˌɔːtə'meɪʃn]	*Automatisierung*	A **automatic** [ˌɔːtə'mætɪk] *automatisch*
rationalization [ˌræʃnəlaɪ'zeɪʃn]	*Rationalisierung*	v **rationalize** (sth.) ['ræʃnəlaɪz] (BE) *rationalisieren; Stellen abbauen (in einem Betrieb usw.)*
invest in sth. [ɪn'vest]	*in etw. investieren*	N **investment** *Investition, Kapitalanlage* N **investor** *Investor/in, Kapitalanleger/in*
8 **reduce costs** [rɪˌdjuːs 'kɒsts]	*(die) Kosten senken*	= **cut/lower costs** ◊ **increase / push up costs** N **reduction** [rɪ'dʌkʃn] *Reduzierung, Senkung* v **cost, cost, cost** *kosten*
9 **maximize profit(s)** [ˌmæksɪmaɪz 'prɒfɪts]	*den Profit maximieren, die Gewinne maximieren*	◊ **minimize loss(es)** ['mɪnɪmaɪz] ❗ stress: **profit** ['--] v **profit from** sth. (fml) *von etw. profitieren* A **profitable** ['prɒfɪtəbl] *gewinnbringend, rentabel*
a multinational company [ˌmʌlti'næʃnəl]	*ein multinationales Unter-nehmen*	= **a global player** ◊ **a national company**
10 **relocate** sth. [ˌriːləʊ'keɪt ☆ ˌriː'ləʊkeɪt]	*etw. verlegen, etw. verlagern*	N **relocation** [ˌriːləʊ'keɪʃn] *Verlegung, Umsiedlung*
outsource sth. ['aʊtsɔːs]	*etw. ausgliedern; etw. nach außen verlagern*	N **outsourcing** ◊ **insourcing / bringing it in-house**
11 **wage** [weɪdʒ], also **wages** (pl)	*(Tages-, Wochen-)Lohn*	**wage demands** *Lohnforderungen* **demand higher wages** *höhere Löhne fordern*

2 Future trends in the job market

Outsourcing labour has, however, led to high unemployment rates at home, especially in the 'traditional' manufacturing
15 industries. At the same time, there has been a growth in the service sector and an increase in part-time and temporary employment. However, many of these jobs in the service sector are low-skilled and low-paid.

20 Most industrialized countries will see their workforces shrink due to low birthrates and will be faced with a shortage of highly skilled workers in the younger generations. Ageing societies may have to reconsider traditional retirement models and give women, especially mothers, better access to work.

Word family 'employ'

V **employ** [ɪmˈplɔɪ] *anstellen, beschäftigen*
A **employable** [ɪmˈplɔɪəbl] *vermittelbar, anstellbar, im Beruf einsetzbar*
N **employer** [ɪmˈplɔɪə] *Arbeitgeber/in, Unternehmer/in*
N **employee** [ɪmˈplɔɪiː] *Arbeitnehmer/in, Angestellte(r), Mitarbeiter/in*
N **employment** [ɪmˈplɔɪmənt] *Beschäftigung, Arbeit, Anstellung*
N **unemployment** *Arbeitslosigkeit*
A **unemployed** *arbeitslos*

Word family 'skill'

N **skill** *Fertigkeit, berufliche Qualifikation*
A **skilful** (BE) / **skillful** (AE) *geschickt*
A **skilled** *ausgebildet, qualifiziert*
A **unskilled** *ungelernt* (Arbeiter, Arbeit)

Collocations with '(un)skilled'

skilled worker *Facharbeiter/in*
highly skilled worker
    hoch qualifizierte(r) Beschäftigte(r)
low-skilled jobs *gering qualifizierte Jobs*
unskilled worker *Hilfsarbeiter/in*
semi-skilled worker
    angelernte(r) Arbeiter/in

13 **unemployment rate**	*Arbeitslosenquote*	◊ **employment rate** *Beschäftigungsquote*
14 **manufacturing industry** [ˌmænjuːˈfæktʃərɪŋˈɪndəstri]	*produzierendes Gewerbe; Fertigungsindustrie*	V **manufacture** [ˌmænjuˈfæktʃə] *herstellen, produzieren* N **manufacturer** *Hersteller (von Gerät usw.)*
16 **service sector** [ˈsɜːvɪsˌsektə]	*Dienstleistungssektor*	**jobs in the service sector** *Dienstleistungsberufe* V **serve** *(be)dienen*
part-time employment	*Teilzeitarbeit*	= **part-time work / a part-time job** ◊ **full-time employment / a full-time job** **work part-time** *(in) Teilzeit arbeiten*
temporary employment [ˈtemprəri ☆ ˈtempəreri]	*vorübergehende Beschäftigung, Zeitarbeit; Aushilfstätigkeit*	= **temporary work / a temporary job** ◊ **permanent employment / a permanent job**
18 **low-paid**	*schlecht bezahlt*	= **badly paid** ◊ **highly paid / well-paid** V **pay** sb./sth. *(Person / Summe, Rechnung) bezahlen* ! **pay for** sth. *(Ware, Leistung) bezahlen* N **pay** *Bezahlung, Lohn, Gehalt*
19 **industrialized country** [ɪnˈdʌstriəlaɪzd]	*Industrieland, Industriestaat*	= **industrial(ized) nation / developed country** A **industrial** [ɪnˈdʌstriəl] *Industrie..., industriell* N **industry** [ˈɪndəstri] *Industrie*
workforce [ˈwɜːkfɔːs] (+ sing or pl verb)	*Belegschaft, Arbeitskräfte*	= **labour force** **force** *Truppe*
22 **retirement model** [rɪˈtaɪəmənt ˌmɒdl]	*Ruhestandsregelung, Pensionierungsregelung*	V **retire** [rɪˈtaɪə] *in Rente / Pension gehen* ! stress: **model** [ˈmɒdl]
23 **access to work** [ˈækses]	*Zugang zum Arbeitsmarkt, Beschäftigungsmöglichkeit*	! **ac**cess [ˈækses] *Zugang, Zugriff* **ex**cess [ɪkˈses] *Übermaß* A **accessible** [əkˈsesəbl] *erreichbar, zugänglich*

3 Changes in the workplace

Until now the work model has been based on a corporate ladder,
25 in which employees were promoted to higher levels in their
company. However, with job security disappearing and hiring
and firing systems becoming more universal, people are less
likely to work for one company for a long period. Moreover, the
old nine-to-five jobs are being replaced by flexitime jobs.

30 In today's rapidly changing high-tech world, employees at all
levels have to be better qualified to find work. Frequent
in-service training is now part of company culture, as firms
seek to meet the demands and challenges of the modern
workplace. Employees must be prepared for repeated
35 professional reorientation.

Working for international companies and in international teams
requires the ability to communicate across cultures in various
languages and use soft skills such as flexibility or empathy.

'We look for people who can quickly adapt to changes in the workplace.'

'qualified' [ˈkwɒlɪfaɪd]

qualified (für den Beruf) *qualifiziert*
well qualified *ausreichend qualifiziert,*
  gut ausgebildet
be fully qualified *eine abgeschlossene*
  Ausbildung haben
be qualified to do sth. *in der Lage sein,*
  etw. zu tun

24 **corporate ladder** ['kɔːpərət]	*Karriereleiter* (in der freien Wirtschaft)	**corporate** *Unternehmens..., Firmen...* **work** one's **way up the (corporate) ladder** *sich hocharbeiten*
25 **promote sb. (to sth.)** [prə'məʊt]	*jdn. (zu etw.) befördern*	N **promotion** [prə'məʊʃn] *Beförderung*
26 **job security** [sə'kjʊərəti]	*Arbeitsplatzgarantie, Arbeitsplatzsicherheit*	◊ **job insecurity** *Arbeitsplatzunsicherheit* **enjoy/have job security** *eine sichere Stelle haben*
hire and fire	*(Personal) nach Bedarf einstellen und kündigen*	= **employ and dismiss people**
29 **a nine-to-five job**	*Arbeit von 9 Uhr morgens bis 5 Uhr nachmittags; Büroarbeit*	**I have a nine-to-five job.** = **I work nine to five.**
a flexitime job ['fleksitaɪm]	*ein Arbeitsplatz mit gleitender (= flexibler) Arbeitszeit*	**flexitime** (BE) = **flextime** (AE) **work flexitime** *gleitende Arbeitszeit(en) haben*
32 **in-service training**	*(eine) innerbetriebliche Fortbildung*	v **train** *ausbilden, trainieren*
33 **meet demands/challenges** [dɪ'mɑːndz, 'tʃælɪndʒɪz]	*Erfordernissen/Herausforderungen gerecht werden*	v **demand** *(er)fordern* v **challenge** *herausfordern*
34 **workplace**	*Arbeitsplatz*	! *Arbeitsplatz =* **1. workplace** *Arbeitsstätte* **in the workplace** *am Arbeitsplatz* **2. job** *Stelle, Stellung* **job creation** *die Schaffung von Arbeitsplätzen*
35 **professional reorientation** [prə,feʃənl ,riːɔːriən'teɪʃn]	*berufliche Neu-/Umorientierung, beruflicher Neuanfang*	N **profession** [prə'feʃn] *(akademischer) Beruf* v **reorient** oneself [,riː'ɔːriənt] *sich neu orientieren*
38 **soft skills**	*Soft Skills (= Kompetenzen im Umgang mit anderen Menschen)*	= **people skills** ◊ **hard skills** *rein fachliche Qualifikationen*

4   Working on the move

At the same time, new electronic gadgets and related
40 technologies have transformed our world – changing how,
where and when we <u>do business</u> – and they have brought a
previously unknown degree of personal freedom to the workplace.

More and more employers are encouraging their employees to
45 work remotely or from home. These 'nomad workers' need
access to corporate information – easily provided by their
smartphones or netbooks – but not necessarily a traditional office
cubicle or even a home office.

'Doing my work from home over the Internet?
You bet I'm interested!'

German 'Geschäfte machen'

<u>do business</u> **with** sb.
  Geschäfte mit jdm. machen
deal in sth. **(dealt, dealt) / make money
  out of** sth.   *Geschäfte / ein Geschäft mit
  etw. machen, Geld mit etw. verdienen*
strike a good deal (struck, struck)
  ein gutes Geschäft machen

41 **do business** ['bɪznəs]	*Geschäfte machen, Handel treiben*	**!** **business** pronunciation: ['bɪznəs = nur 2 Silben] 1. *Geschäfte, Handel* (**How's business?**); 2. *Unternehmen, Firma* (**a business**); 3. *Aufgabe, Sache, Verantwortung* (**Mind your own business.**)
45 **work remotely** [rɪ'məʊtli]	*ortsunabhängig arbeiten; von unterwegs aus arbeiten*	A **remote** *abgelegen, fern*
work from home	*von zu Hause (aus) arbeiten*	**!** **work away from home** *auswärts arbeiten* (z.B. auf Montage), *fern von daheim arbeiten*
nomad worker ['nəʊmæd]	*Telearbeiter/in (der/die zu Hause und an anderen Orten unter Zugriff auf das Kommunikationsnetz des Arbeitgebers arbeitet)*	= **teleworker** **nomad** *Nomade/-in (= Angehörige(r) eines Wandervolkes)* **!** stress: **nomad** ['--]
48 **office cubicle** ['kju:bɪkl] (esp. AE)	*Bürozelle; abgeschirmter Platz in einem Großraumbüro*	
home office	*häusliches Arbeitszimmer, Heimbüro*	**!** **home office** 1. *Heimbüro;* 2. *Zentrale, Hauptsitz* (einer Firma); 3. **the Home Office** *das britische Innenministerium*

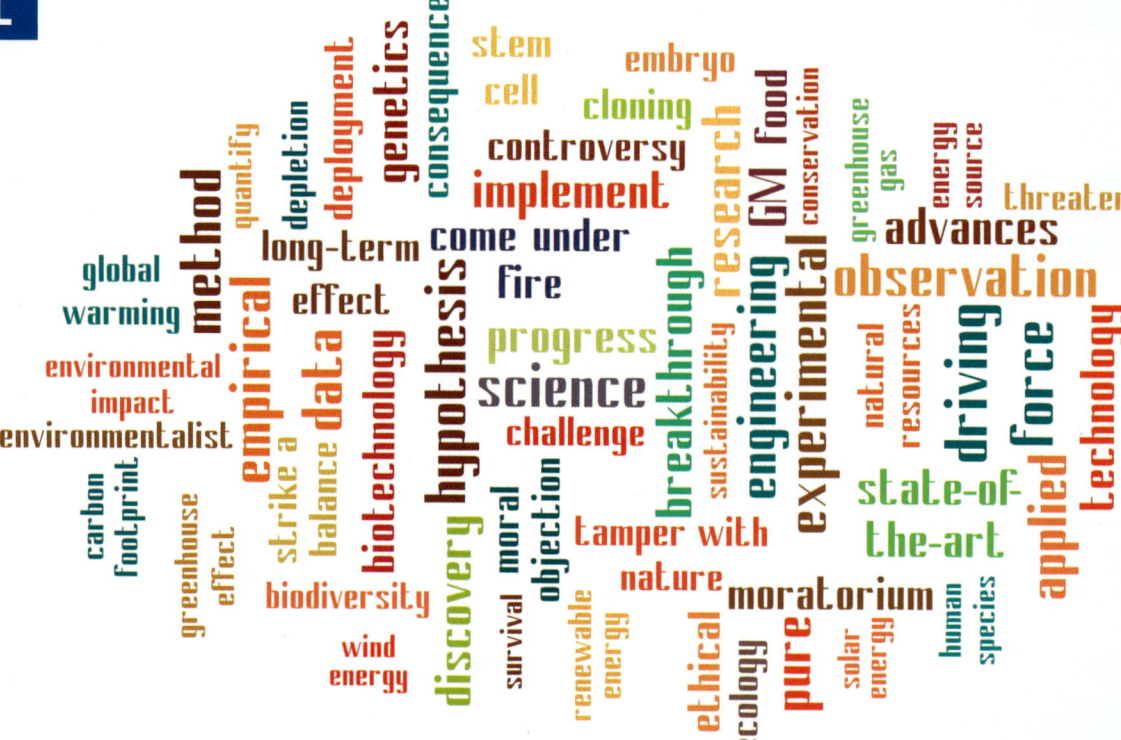

Science, Technology and the Environment

1 Scientific fields

The last century saw <u>science</u> and technology emerge as one of the driving forces of modern civilization. The experimental method, based on hypothesis, close observation, and the collection of empirical data, has led to a veritable revolution in our way of life.

While <u>pure science</u> engages in basic research, pushing back the frontiers of human knowledge, the <u>applied sciences</u> and engineering concentrate on implementing new discoveries. These have resulted in major advances in communication, transport and many other fields.

Breakthroughs in medicine and physics, for example, have made it possible for people to live longer and healthier lives than ever before, but also to destroy all life on the planet at the push of a button. Yet few people doubt the necessity of continued progress, and the use of state-of-the-art technology is considered essential for success in the global economy.

Word family 'science'

N <u>science</u> ['saɪəns] *(Natur-)Wissenschaft, naturwissenschaftliche Disziplin*

N **scientist** ['saɪəntɪst] *(Natur-)Wissenschaftler/in*

A **scientific** [ˌsaɪən'tɪfɪk] *(natur)wissenschaftlich; exakt*

Collocations with 'science'

<u>pure science</u> [pjʊə] *theoretische Wissenschaft, reine Wissenschaft*

<u>applied science</u> *angewandte Wissenschaft*

life sciences *Biowissenschaften (= Biologie, Medizin usw.)*

science fiction [ˌ‑‑ '‑‑] *Science-Fiction*
science park ['‑‑ ‑] *Technologiepark, Wissenschaftszentrum*

CHECKPOINT — *In English, please!*

a *eine regelrechte Revolution auslösen*
b *die Grenzen des menschlichen Wissens ausdehnen*
c *zu großen Fortschritten auf vielen Gebieten führen*
d *alles Leben auf Knopfdruck zerstören*

2 **the driving force**	*die treibende Kraft*	**force** 1. *Kraft, Macht;* 2. *Gewalt;* 3. *Truppe*
the experimental method [ɪkˌsperɪˌmentl 'meθəd]	*die experimentelle (Prüf-) Methode*	N|V **experiment** [ɪk'sperɪmənt] 1. *Experiment, Versuch;* 2. *experimentieren, Versuche anstellen*
3 **hypothesis** [haɪ'pɒθəsɪs], pl **hypotheses** [haɪ'pɒθəsiːz]	*Hypothese, Annahme*	! stress: **hypothesis** [-'---] A **hypothetical** [ˌhaɪpə'θetɪkl] *hypothetisch*
close observation [ˌkləʊsˌɒbzə'veɪʃn]	*genaue/eingehende Beobachtung*	! A **close** [kləʊs] – V **close** [kləʊz] *schließen* V **observe** [əb'zɜːv] *beobachten*
4 **empirical data** (pl, fml) [ɪmˌpɪrɪkl 'deɪtə]	*empirische Daten (= durch Beobachtung oder Experiment gewonnene Daten)*	**empirical** ◆ **theoretical** [ˌθɪə'retɪkl] **collect/gather data** *Daten sammeln/erfassen*
6 **basic research** [rɪ'sɜːtʃ, 'riːsɜːtʃ]	*Grundlagenforschung*	N **basis** ['beɪsɪs] *Basis, Grundlage* V **research** [rɪ'sɜːtʃ] *erforschen, untersuchen*
8 **engineering** [ˌendʒɪ'nɪərɪŋ]	*Ingenieurwesen; Technik und Konstruktion*	**mechanical engineering** *Maschinenbau* N **engineer** [ˌendʒɪ'nɪə] *Ingenieur/in*
implement new discoveries ['ɪmplɪmənt, dɪ'skʌvəriz]	*neue Entdeckungen in die Tat umsetzen, neue Erkenntnisse anwenden*	N **implementation** [ˌɪmplɪmen'teɪʃn] *Ausführung, Durchführung, Einführung (und Anwendung)* V **discover** *entdecken*
9 **major advances** [ˌmeɪdʒər əd'vɑːnsɪz]	*große Fortschritte*	**major** *groß, bedeutend, wesentlich* A **advanced** *fortgeschritten*
11 **breakthrough** ['breɪkθruː]	*Durchbruch*	V **break through** [ˌ-'-] *einen Durchbruch machen*
15 **progress** (no pl) ['prəʊgres ☆ 'prɑːgrəs]	*Fortschritt(e)*	**make progress** *Fortschritte machen* V **progress** [prə'gres] *Fortschritte machen*
state-of-the-art technology [tek'nɒlədʒi]	*modernste Technik; Technik auf dem neuesten Stand*	= **The technology is state of the art.** (no hyphen!) ! *Technik (= Fertigkeit, Methode)* = **technique** [tek'niːk]

2 Genetic research

In recent years, the life sciences, especially genetics and biotechnology, have come under fire for ethical reasons. Critics of genetically modified (GM) food, for example, often call for a
20 moratorium on the deployment of GM food for as long as the long-term effects have not been sufficiently investigated. Introducing artificially created plants into the environment could have unforeseen consequences, they warn.

The controversy surrounding stem cell research and cloning is
25 based on more general moral objections: it is felt to be wrong for humans to tamper with nature and to destroy human embryos as part of the process.

Word family 'gene'

N **gene** [dʒiːn] *Gen, Erbfaktor*
A **genetic** [dʒə'netɪk] *genetisch, Gen…*
ADV **genetically** *genetisch*
N **genetics** [dʒə'netɪks] *Genetik, Vererbungslehre*
N **genome** ['dʒiːnəʊm] *Genom, Erbgut*

Collocations with 'genetic(ally)'

genetic code *genetischer Kode*
genetic disorder *genetische Störung*
genetic engineering *Gentechnologie, Gentechnik*
genetic fingerprint ['fɪŋgəprɪnt] *genetischer Fingerabdruck*

genetically modified (abbr. **GM**) *genetisch verändert, genmanipuliert*
genetically modified food *Genfood, genetisch veränderte Lebensmittel*

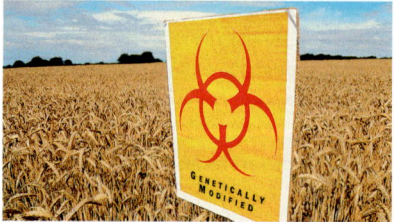

CHECKPOINT — *In English, please!*

a *aus ethischen Gründen ins Kreuzfeuer der Kritik geraten*
b *die Langzeitfolgen hinreichend untersuchen*
c *künstlich geschaffene Pflanzen in die Umwelt einbringen*
d *es für falsch halten, dass Menschen menschliche Embryos zerstören*

18 **biotechnology** [ˌbaɪəʊtek'nɒlədʒi]	*Biotechnologie, Biotechnik*	**bio-** ['baɪəʊ] = connected with living things or human life
come under fire	*unter Beschuss geraten, ins Kreuzfeuer der Kritik geraten*	= 1. be shot at; 2. be criticized severely for what you have done
ethical ['eθɪkl]	*moralisch, ethisch*	N **ethics** ['eθɪks] *Ethik, moralische Prinzipien*
19 **call for a moratorium (on sth.)** [ˌmɒrə'tɔːriəm]	*die vorläufige Einstellung (von etw.) fordern, einen Aufschub fordern*	**moratorium** = a stopping of an activity for a period of time, especially by official agreement
20 **deployment** [dɪ'plɔɪment]	*Einsatz, Verteilung, Entwicklung*	V **deploy** *einsetzen, anwenden, entwickeln*
21 **long-term effects** [ɪ'fekts]	*Langzeitfolgen, -wirkungen*	◊ **short-term effects** *kurzfristige Auswirkungen*
23 **unforeseen consequences** [ˌʌnfɔː,siːn 'kɒnsɪkwənsɪz]	*ungeahnte Folgen, nicht vorhersehbare Auswirkungen*	= **unexpected consequences** *unerwartete Folgen* ◊ **foreseeable consequences** *vorhersehbare Folgen*
24 **controversy** ['kɒntrəvɜːsi, BE also: kən'trɒvəsi]	*Auseinandersetzung; Streit*	a controversy over/about/surrounding sth. A **controversial** [ˌkɒntrə'vɜːʃl] *umstritten, kontrovers*
stem cell research ['stem sel]	*Stammzellenforschung*	blood/brain/nerve cell *Blut-/Gehirn-/Nervenzelle*
cloning ['kləʊnɪŋ]	*Klonen, Klonierung*	V|N **clone** 1. *klonen;* 2. *Klon*
25 **a moral objection** [ˌmɒrəl_əb'dʒekʃn]	*ein moralischer Einwand*	**!** stress: **mor**al ['--] N **morals** (pl) *Moral(vorstellungen)* V **object to** [əb'dʒekt] *Einwände haben gegen*
26 **tamper with nature** ['neɪtʃə]	*der Natur ins Handwerk pfuschen; die Natur manipulieren*	**!** stress: **na**ture ['--] No article: **tamper with nature** A **natural** ['nætʃrəl] *natürlich, Natur...*
embryo ['embrɪəʊ]	*Embryo, noch nicht geborenes Lebewesen*	= **foetus** (BE) / **fetus** (AE) ['fiːtəs] *Fetus, Fötus*

3 Ecology

One of the major challenges facing us in the 21st century is
striking a balance between economy and ecology. As global
30 warming, the gradual depletion of natural resources, and the
loss of biodiversity threaten the existence of life on our planet,
environmentalists are calling for a radical change in our
attitudes. To quantify the environmental impact of human
activities, they have invented the term 'carbon footprint': the
35 larger the carbon footprint, the more a certain activity
contributes to the greenhouse effect.

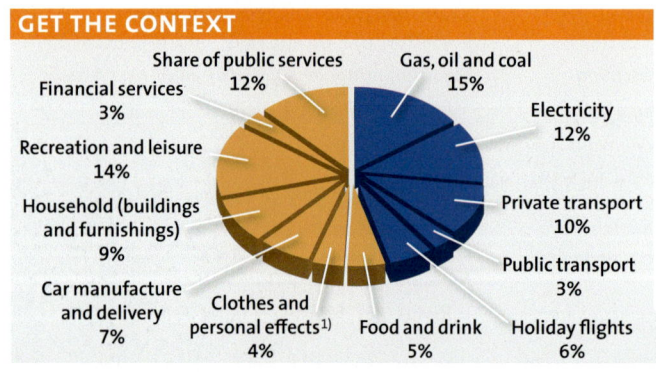

GET THE CONTEXT

Share of public services 12%
Financial services 3%
Recreation and leisure 14%
Household (buildings and furnishings) 9%
Car manufacture and delivery 7%
Clothes and personal effects[1] 4%
Food and drink 5%
Gas, oil and coal 15%
Electricity 12%
Private transport 10%
Public transport 3%
Holiday flights 6%

■ indirectly caused emissions
■ directly caused emissions

[1] personal effects (pl, fml) *persönliche Gegenstände*

Breakdown of a typical person's
carbon footprint in the developed world

28 **a major challenge** [ˌmeɪdʒə 'tʃælɪndʒ]	*eine große Herausforderung, eine enorme Herausforderung*	V **challenge** *herausfordern*
29 **strike a balance (between** A **and** B**)** ['bæləns], **struck, struck**	*den Mittelweg finden, das richtige Verhältnis (zwischen A und B) finden*	**balance** *Gleichgewicht* ◆ **imbalance** *Ungleichgewicht* **!** stress: **balance** ['--]
ecology [ɪ'kɒlədʒi]	*Ökologie*	**!** stress: **ecology** [-'---] A **ecological** [ˌiːkə'lɒdʒɪkl] *ökologisch, Umwelt...*
global warming ['gləʊbl]	*die globale Erwärmung, die Erwärmung der Erdatmosphäre*	N **globe** *Welt(kugel), Erde*
30 **the depletion of natural resources** [dɪ'pliːʃn, ˌnætʃrəl rɪ'sɔːsɪz]	*der Raubbau an natürlichen Ressourcen; der massive Abbau natürlicher Ressourcen*	V **be depleted** [dɪ'pliːtɪd] (fml) *(von Vorräten)* *verbraucht sein, erschöpft sein*
31 **the loss of biodiversity** [ˌbaɪəʊdaɪ'vɜːsəti]	*der Verlust der Artenvielfalt, die Abnahme der biologischen Vielfalt*	V **lose, lost, lost** *verlieren* **!** **loss** [lɒs] – **lose** [luːz] – **loose** [luːs] *lose, locker* **conserve biodiversity** [kən'sɜːv] *die Artenvielfalt erhalten*
threaten sb./sth. ['θretn]	*jdn./etw. bedrohen*	= **be a threat/danger to** sb./sth.
33 **quantify** sth. ['kwɒntɪfaɪ]	*etw. messen, etw. quantifizieren*	N **quantity** ['kwɒntəti] *Menge, Quantität*
34 **carbon footprint** [ˌkɑːbən 'fʊtprɪnt]	*CO₂-Fußabdruck, CO₂-Bilanz*	**reduce (the size of) your carbon footprint** *den eigenen CO₂-Fußabdruck verringern, die CO₂-Bilanz verbessern* **carbon dioxide** [daɪ'ɒksaɪd] *Kohlendioxid (CO₂)*
36 **the greenhouse effect** ['griːnhaʊs_ɪˌfekt]	*der Treibhauseffekt*	**greenhouse** *Gewächshaus, Treibhaus* **!** **effect** [ɪ'fekt] *(Aus-)Wirkung, Effekt* **affect** sth. [ə'fekt] *sich auf etw. auswirken*

4 Sustainability

Sustainability has become the keyword of the new century: the reduction of greenhouse gases, the implementation of renewable energy sources (e.g. solar and wind energy), and
40 conservation of our natural resources have come to be regarded as essential for the survival of the human species.

It remains to be seen whether science, having profoundly changed life on this planet, will
45 successfully rise to the challenge of dealing with the consequences of our technical civilization.

CHECKPOINT — *In English, please!*

a *die Verringerung von Treibhausgasen*
b *die Einführung und Anwendung erneuerbarer Energien*
c *die Erhaltung unserer natürlichen Ressourcen*
d *das Leben auf diesem Planeten grundlegend verändern*

Collocations with 'energy'

! stress: **energy** ['---]
renewable energy [rɪ'njuːəbl]
erneuerbare Energie
alternative energy [ɔːl'tɜːnətɪv]
alternative Energie(formen)
solar energy ['səʊlə]
Solarenergie, Sonnenenergie
wind energy [wɪnd]
Windenergie
wave energy
Wellenenergie, Energie aus Wellenkraft
nuclear/atomic energy ['njuːklɪə, ə'tɒmɪk]
Kernenergie, Atomkraft

conserve/save energy
Energie (ein)sparen
consume/use energy
Energie verbrauchen
waste energy
Energie verschwenden
generate/produce energy
Energie erzeugen

the demand for energy
der Energiebedarf, die Nachfrage nach Energie

37 **sustainability** [sə,steɪnə'bɪləti]	*Nachhaltigkeit, nachhaltige Entwicklung*	A **sustainable** [sə'steɪnəbl] *nachhaltig; umweltgerecht*
38 **greenhouse gas** [gæs]	*Treibhausgas*	**greenhouse gas emissions** [i'mɪʃnz] *Treibhausgasemissionen*
39 **renewable energy sources** ['enədʒi ,sɔːsɪz]	*erneuerbare Energiequellen, erneuerbare Energieträger*	V **renew** *erneuern* N **renewal** [rɪ'njuːəl] *Erneuerung* ! homophones: **source** *Quelle* – **sauce** [sɔːs] *Soße*
40 **conservation** [,kɒnsə'veɪʃn]	*(Natur-)Schutz, Erhaltung*	**conservation area** *Naturschutzgebiet* N **conservationist** [,kɒnsə'veɪʃənɪst] *Naturschützer/in, Umweltschützer/in* V **conserve** [kən'sɜːv] *(Energie usw.) sparen*
41 **the survival of the human species** [sə'vaɪvl, ,hjuːmən 'spiːʃiːz]	*das Überleben der Gattung Mensch*	V **survive** [sə'vaɪv] *überleben* N **survivor** [sə'vaɪvə] *Überlebende(r); Überlebenskünstler/in* A|N **human** 1. *menschlich, Menschen...;* 2. *Mensch* ! stress: <u>human</u> ['--] pronunciation: **species** ['spiːʃiːz] *Art, Spezies* sing and pl the same: **one species** – **two species**
45 **rise to the challenge** ['tʃælɪndʒ], **rose, risen** ['rɪzn]	*sich der Herausforderung stellen, sich der Herausforderung gewachsen zeigen*	V **challenge** *herausfordern*
46 **deal with the consequences of** sth. ['kɒnsɪkwənsɪz], **dealt** [delt], **dealt**	*mit den Folgen von etw. umgehen*	**deal with** 1. *fertigwerden mit, sich kümmern um;* 2. *handeln von (= zum Inhalt haben)* ! stress: <u>consequence</u> ['---] **suffer/face/take the consequences** *die Konsequenzen/Folgen (er)tragen*

TWEETING ADVERT

SOCIAL
NETWORKING

INFORMATION SHARING COMMERCIAL TELEVISION ELECTRONIC BROADCASTING INVASION OF PRIVACY DIGITAL CORPORATION

PARTICIPATORY MEDIA SMARTPHONE STAFF BROADBAND

MEDIA LITERACY MEDIA GURU

PROGRAMME

BROADCASTING

COMMERCIALS

BIG SPONSOR

MEDIA

ADVERTISING REVENUE NET BROADCASTING DOWNLOAD BUSINESS COMMUNICATION ILLEGAL DISSEMINATION

FILE SHARING COPYRIGHT INFRINGEMENT PRINT

USER-GENERATED
CONTENT

BLOGGING
ANONYMITY

PUBLISHING
HOUSE

TARGET GROUP INTERNET ACCESS ACCESSIBILITY STORE

PERIODICAL MASS CRITIC NETWORK MAINSTREAM ADVERTISER

CHANNEL WEB 2.0 IDENTITY THEFT

EMPOWERMENT MEDIA

PROGRAMMING

MEDIUM MEDIA HYPE

The Media

1 The development of the mass media

In the broadest sense of the word, the media are channels of communication and thus as old as human culture itself.

Mass media in the modern sense first came into existence in the second half of the 19th century, when new developments in
5 printing and papermaking made it possible to print large quantities of written information quickly and at low cost.

In the 1930s, the print media had to compete with new forms of media such as radio and, from the 1950s onwards, television. Within a few decades, the new electronic media had conquered
10 living rooms throughout the Western world.

Radio in 1945: a medium for the masses
(cf. entry 'medium' on p. 139)

CHECKPOINT — *In English, please!*

a erstmals im 19. Jahrhundert entstehen
b es möglich machen, große Mengen zu drucken
c mit neuen Medien(formen) konkurrieren müssen
d die Wohnzimmer in der ganzen westlichen Welt erobern

'the media' + plural or singular verb

The plural expression **the media** (meaning 'radio, TV, newspapers, the Internet') is sometimes used with a singular verb:

> The media *were/was* involved in the story.
> *Die Medien waren an der Geschichte beteiligt.*

1 **channel of communication** [kə‚mjuːnɪˈkeɪʃn]	*Kommunikationsweg, Kommunikationskanal*	V **communicate** [kəˈmjuːnɪkeɪt] *kommunizieren* ❗ *Kanal (= künstlicher Wasserweg)* = **canal** [kəˈnæl]
3 **the mass media** [‚mæs ˈmiːdiə]	*die Massenmedien*	= the Internet, television, newspapers, magazines, film and radio
7 **the print media**	*die Printmedien; auch: die Presse*	= newspapers, magazines and books V **print** *drucken* N **(colour/laser/inkjet) printer** *(Farb-/Laser-/Tintenstrahl-)Drucker*
9 **the electronic media** [ɪ‚lekˈtrɒnɪk]	*die elektronischen Medien*	= media, e.g. the Internet, that use electronics to reach their audience

■ **printing press** *Druckerpresse, Druckmaschine*

The printing press, invented by Johannes Gutenberg around 1450, revolutionized the way books were made. Before Gutenberg, all books were copied by hand. Gutenberg combined movable type (individual letters made of lead[1]) with a mechanical press, making it possible to print any page as often as desired with little additional effort. As a result, books became more accessible, and the number of titles rose rapidly.

[1] **lead** [led] *Blei*

■ **The changing news landscape**

Americans who read a daily newspaper the previous day

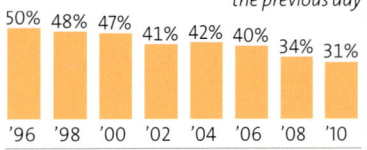

'96	'98	'00	'02	'04	'06	'08	'10
50%	48%	47%	41%	42%	40%	34%	31%

Americans who got news online the previous day

'04	'06	'08	'10
24%	23%	29%	34%

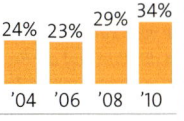

2 Financing (mass) media

Requiring a large staff and considerable technical support, the media have traditionally remained the property of big business: publishing houses or broadcasting corporations (called networks in the USA). These private firms finance their operations through
15 advertising revenue, i.e. by selling either space for adverts in periodicals or broadcasting time for commercials on radio or TV. On commercially operated television, sponsors may exert influence on the content of the programmes in which their commercials are shown. Programming can be designed to
20 appeal to a certain target group of particular interest to the advertiser.

CHECKPOINT — *In English, please!*

a *sich durch Werbeeinnahmen finanzieren*
b *Einfluss auf die Programminhalte nehmen/ausüben*
c *eine bestimmte Zielgruppe ansprechen*
d *von besonderem Interesse für den Werbenden sein*

11 **staff** (+ sing or pl verb) [stɑːf ☆ stæf]	*Mitarbeiter(stab), Personal(bestand), Belegschaft*	**The staff are** (BE) **/ is** (AE) **on strike.** *Die Mitarbeiter streiken.* **!** *ein/e Mitarbeiter/in* = **a member of staff** (BE) *alle Mitarbeiter/innen* = **all staff**
12 **big business**	*die großen Konzerne, die Groß-industrie*	**links between politics and big business**
13 **publishing house** [ˈpʌblɪʃɪŋ]	*Verlag(shaus)*	= **publisher** v **publish** *veröffentlichen, herausbringen*
broadcasting corporation (BE) [ˌbrɔːdkɑːstɪŋ ˌkɔːpəˈreɪʃn] = **broadcast(ing) network** (AE)	*Sendeanstalt, Rundfunkanstalt*	= **(radio/TV) station** v **broadcast, broadcast, broadcast** (im Radio, Fernsehen) *senden* **the BBC** = **the British Broadcasting Corporation**
15 **advertising revenue** [ˌædvətaɪzɪŋ ˈrevənjuː]	*Werbeeinnahmen*	**tax revenue** *Steueraufkommen, Steuereinnahmen (des Staates)*
16 **periodical** [ˌpɪəriˈɒdɪkl]	*Fachzeitschrift, Journal*	= **magazine** [ˌmægəˈziːn ☆ ˈmægəziːn] N **period** [ˈpɪəriəd] *Zeit, Zeitraum*
broadcasting time	*Sendezeit*	= **airtime**
17 **commercially operated television (TV)** [ˈɒpəreɪtɪd]	*kommerziell betriebenes Fernsehen, Privatfernsehen*	= **commercial television (TV)** ◊ **public (service) television** *das öffentlich-rechtliche Fernsehen* N **commerce** [ˈkɒmɜːs] *Handel (als Wirtschaftszweig)*
sponsor [ˈspɒnsə]	*Sponsor/in, Förderer/-in, Geldgeber/in*	**!** pronunciation: **sponsor** [ˈspɒnsə] v **sponsor** *sponsern, fördern, unterstützen* N **sponsorship** *finanzielle Unterstützung, Sponsoring*
20 **target group** [ˈtɑːgɪt]	*Zielgruppe*	**target** *Ziel(scheibe)*

3   The Internet and its digital revolution

In the last decade of the 20th century, the Internet emerged as a powerful new medium. Originally simply a network of computers located in various places throughout the world, the
25 Internet has become the mainstream channel for all manner of content. This was made possible by the digital revolution that reduced media content of almost any sort (texts, images, audio and video clips) to a stream of bits and bytes that can be copied, stored, and sent round the world at will.

30 New forms of information sharing and dissemination have emerged since the spread of broadband Internet access: blogging, tweeting, file sharing and social networking are only four of the many new applications that have been created.

Because anyone with Internet access via computer or
35 smartphone can upload user-generated content to the Net, some observers see a fundamental change from the mass-media era of the last century to the era of participatory media in the 21st century.

Collocations with 'digital' ['dɪdʒɪtl]

the digital revolution [ˌrevəˈluːʃn]
die digitale Revolution
the digital divide *die digitale Spaltung*
(zwischen regelmäßigen Internet-
nutzern und Nicht-Internetnutzern)
digital signature ['sɪgnətʃə]
digital radio/television
DVD (= digital versatile disc ['vɜːsətaɪl]**)**

'content' ['kɒntent] – **'contents'**

content **1.** *Gehalt, enthaltener Anteil;*
2. *Inhalt(e) einer Website, CD-ROM usw.;*
3. *wesentlicher Kern, (gedanklicher)
Inhalt* (eines Buchs, Films usw.)

contents (pl) **1.** *Inhalt* (allgemein);
2. *Inhaltsverzeichnis* (**table of contents**)
❗ *Inhaltsangabe* = **summary**

CHECKPOINT   *In English, please!*

a *sich als mächtiges neues Medium
   entpuppen/erweisen*
b *Medieninhalte nach Belieben kopieren*
c *Internetzugang über einen Computer oder
   ein Smartphone haben*
d *nutzergenerierte Inhalte ins Netz
   hochladen*

23 **medium** ['miːdiəm], pl **media** ['miːdiə]	*(Kommunikations-)Medium*	**media library** *Mediathek* **media content** *Medieninhalte*
network	*Netzwerk; Sendernetz*	**local area network (LAN)** *lokales Netzwerk*
25 **mainstream** ['meɪnstriːm]	*für die breite Masse*	**main** *Haupt...*
29 **store** sth.	*(Informationen) speichern*	**!** *eine Datei speichern (= sichern)* = **save a file**
30 **information sharing**	*Informationsaustausch*	v **share** sth. *sich etw. teilen, etw. austauschen*
dissemination [dɪˌsemɪˈneɪʃn]	*Verbreitung; Veröffentlichung*	v **disseminate** [dɪˈsemɪneɪt] *verbreiten, ausstreuen*
31 **broadband Internet access** [ˌbrɔːdbænd_ˌɪntənet_ˈækses]	*Breitband-Internetzugang, Breitbandanschluss*	= **high-speed Internet access** v **access the Internet** *auf das Internet zugreifen*
32 **blogging**	*(das) Bloggen*	**start/write/post/read/update a blog**
tweet	*twittern, Twitter nutzen*	N **tweet** *Tweet, Twitternachricht*
file sharing	*der Austausch von Dateien über ein Datennetz, Filesharing*	**file 1.** *Datei;* **2.** *Akte;* **3.** *Aktenordner*
social networking [ˌsəʊʃl ˈnetwɜːkɪŋ]	*die Kommunikation mittels sozialer Netzwerke*	**!** *soziale Netzwerke* = **online social networks** or **social networking (web)sites/services**
35 **smartphone**	*Smartphone*	**smart** *clever, schlau; intelligent*
user-generated content [ˈjuːzə ˈdʒenəreɪtɪd]	*von Benutzern erstellter Inhalt bzw. erstellte Inhalte*	v **use** [juːz] *verwenden, benutzen* N **use** [juːs] *Verwendung, Gebrauch*
37 **participatory media** [pɑːˌtɪsɪˈpeɪtəri ☆ pɑːrˈtɪsəpətɔːri]	*partizipatorische Medien; Medien, die man selbst mitgestaltet*	v **participate in** sth. [pɑːˈtɪsɪpeɪt] *sich an etw. beteiligen, bei etw. mitmachen* N **participation** [pɑːˌtɪsɪˈpeɪʃn] *Teilnahme, Beteiligung* N **participant** [pɑːˈtɪsɪpənt] *Teilnehmer/in*

4 Participatory media: pros and cons

Whereas mass-media content comes from centralized sources
40 dominated by big business, the sources of content for the
participatory media are localized and financially autonomous.
The Internet is thus hailed by some as a tool of individual
empowerment in the hand of the individual. Critics, on the other
hand, warn of the dangers resulting from the anonymity and
45 accessibility of the Net: invasion of privacy, identity theft and
copyright infringement through illegal downloading.

It remains to be seen whether the user-based Internet,
sometimes referred to as Web 2.0, really constitutes a revolution
in the way we live, work and relate to each other, or whether the
50 exaggerated prophecies of media gurus are nothing more than
media hype.

One thing is sure, however:
media literacy is now more
important than ever for
55 those who wish to
successfully navigate the
new media landscape.

*'Illiterate? Can't read? – Just send
for our free brochure ...'*

43 **empowerment** [ɪm'paʊəmənt]	*Ermächtigung, Befähigung; Mitwirkungsfähigkeit*	v **empower** sb. *jdn. ermächtigen, jdn. bevollmächtigen, jdn. befähigen*
44 **anonymity** [ˌænə'nɪməti]	*Anonymität*	A **anonymous** [ə'nɒnɪməs] *anonym*
45 **the accessibility of the Net** [əkˌsesə'bɪləti]	*die (ständige) Zugänglichkeit/ Erreichbarkeit des Internets*	A **accessible** [ək'sesəbl] *zugänglich, erreichbar* N **access** ['ækses] *Zugang*
invasion of privacy [ɪnˌveɪʒn_əv 'prɪvəsi ☆ 'praɪvəsi]	*Verletzung der Privatsphäre, Eingriff in die Privatsphäre*	v **invade** [ɪn'veɪd] *einmarschieren in, einfallen in* A **private** ['praɪvət] *privat*
identity theft [aɪ'dentəti θeft]	*Identitätsdiebstahl (= die missbräuchliche Nutzung personenbezogener Daten)*	v **identify** [aɪ'dentɪfaɪ] *identifizieren* N **thief** [θiːf] *Dieb/in*
46 **copyright infringement** [ˌkɒpiraɪt_ɪn'frɪndʒmənt]	*Urheberrechtsverletzung*	v **infringe on** sth. (fml) (Gesetz, Vertrag usw.) *brechen, verletzen*
illegal downloading [ɪˌliːgl ˌdaʊn'ləʊdɪŋ, 'daʊnləʊdɪŋ]	*illegales Herunterladen*	◊ **legal downloading** ['liːgl] v|N **download 1.** *herunterladen, downloaden;* **2.** ['daʊnləʊd] *Herunterladen, Download*
48 **Web 2.0** [ˌweb tuː pɔɪnt_'əʊ]	*das Web 2.0*	= **the Internet as a participatory medium**
50 **a media guru** ['guːruː]	*ein Medienguru*	**guru** (infml) = **somebody who knows a lot about a particular subject and gives advice**
51 **media hype** [haɪp] (infml, disapproving)	*Medienhype; Medienrummel*	v **hype** sth. (infml, disapproving) *einen Werberummel um etw. veranstalten*
53 **media literacy** ['lɪtərəsi]	*Medienkompetenz (= die Fähigkeit, Medien sinnvoll zu nutzen)*	**literacy** *die Fähigkeit zu lesen und zu schreiben* ◊ **illiteracy** A **literate** ['lɪtərət] *gebildet; belesen* **be literate** *lesen und schreiben können*

Black
official
lingua
creole
convey
ending
English
language
franca
antagonism
protective
promote
word
spread of
gender
measures
communication
colonialism
English
contact
communication
hegemony
order
language
technology
auxiliary
vocabulary
global
lexical
modal
linguistic
dominant
preposition
case
invasion
imperialism
language
language
auxiliary
linguistic
language
speech
inflection
diversity
system
community
variety
ethnic
extinct
cultural
grammar
mother
identification
diversity
proficiency
tongue
Germanic
educator
meaning
endanger
mark
pidgin
hamper

The World of English

1 Features of the English language

It has been claimed that two features of the English language have enabled it to become a global language: its vast vocabulary and its relatively 'simple' grammar. For example, the method of marking the plural by adding an 's' has replaced the Germanic plural based on different endings. In the development of English, inflection lost its function: there are no inflections for gender or case. Instead, auxiliaries, modal auxiliaries, prepositions and a fixed word order are used to convey meaning.

GET THE CONTEXT

■ **Old English** (also: **Anglo-Saxon** *Angelsächsisch*)
The following sentence is from a 10th-century text about the origins of the English language.

> Cōmon hī of þrim folcum ðām strangestan Germānie,
> þæt [is] of Seaxum and of Angle and of Gēatum.
> 'They came from three peoples from the most powerful Germany,
> that is from the Saxons, the Angles and the Jutes.'

Old English contains several symbols which no longer exist in English:
þ and ð were special letters for modern 'th'. In these examples they are both pronounced [θ]. æ was pronounced like [æ].

Old English	Modern English
þrie folc of þrim folcum	three peoples from three peoples
hē cōm hī cōmon	he came they came
se stān sēo tīd þæt folc	the stone the time the people

2 **a global language** [ˌgləʊbl ˈlæŋgwɪdʒ]	*eine Weltsprache*	= **a world language / a universal language** N **globe** *Welt, Erde; Globus*
a vast vocabulary [vɑːst]	*ein umfangreiches Vokabular, ein großer Wortschatz*	= **an extensive / a wide vocabulary** ◑ **a limited vocabulary** *ein begrenztes Vokabular*
3 **grammar** [ˈgræmə]	*Grammatik*	A **grammatical** [grəˈmætɪkl] *grammatisch* N **grammarian** [grəˈmeəriən] *Grammatiker/in*
4 **mark** sth.	*etw. kennzeichnen; etw. markieren*	N **mark** *Zeichen, Markierung; Merkmal* **quotation marks** *Anführungszeichen, -striche*
5 **Germanic** [dʒɜːˈmænɪk]	*germanisch, zur germanischen Sprachfamilie gehörend*	! **Germanic** [-ʹ--] *germanisch* **German** [ʹ--] *deutsch*
ending	*Endung*	V **end in** sth. *auf/mit etw. enden*
6 **inflection** (BE also **inflexion**) [ɪnˈflekʃn]	*Flexion (= Deklination oder Konjugation eines Wortes); Flexionsendung*	V **inflect** [ɪnˈflekt] *flektieren, beugen*
7 **gender** [ˈdʒendə]	*Genus, (grammatisches) Geschlecht*	= **the system of marking words as masculine** [ˈmæskjəlɪn], **feminine** [ˈfemənɪn] **or neuter** [ˈnjuːtə]
case [keɪs]	*Kasus, Fall, Beugungsfall*	**case endings** *Kasusendungen*
auxiliary (verb) [ɔːgˈzɪliəri]	*Hilfsverb*	examples: **be, have, do; will, can, must**
modal auxiliary (verb) [ˈməʊdl]	*Modalverb*	examples: **can, could, may, must**
8 **preposition** [ˌprepəˈzɪʃn]	*Präposition*	examples: **after, at, in, next to, under**
a fixed word order [fɪkst]	*eine feste Wortstellung im Satz; eine feste Satz(glied)stellung*	V **fix** *befestigen; festlegen* **order** *Reihenfolge, Ordnung*
9 **convey meaning** [kənˈveɪ]	*(die) Bedeutung übermitteln, den Sinn ausdrücken*	V **mean, meant** [ment], **meant** *bedeuten* ! *Meinung* = **opinion**

2 English-based pidgins and creoles

10 The process of colonization and the expansion of the British Empire as well as the USA's global role in politics, economy and culture in the 20th century are the most important factors which governed the spread of English. It was colonialism in particular which led to the development of independent
15 varieties of English and to numerous English-based pidgins and creoles.

A pidgin, also known as a contact language, is a language created for communication among people who do not share a common language. A pidgin might gradually expand and
20 extend its grammar to become the mother tongue of a group of people. In this way a pidgin becomes a creole – the language of ethnic identification for a particular speech community. Creole languages developed on slave plantations and became the source of Black English in the USA.

Ferry landing sign (in Vanuatu in the South Pacific): 'If you want the ferry to come, strike the gong.'

German 'Sprach...'

a language course *ein Sprachkurs*
a language holiday *eine Sprachreise*
language use = usage ['juːsɪdʒ, 'juːzɪdʒ]
    Sprachgebrauch
have a feeling for (the) language
    Sprachgefühl haben
a speech community [kə'mjuːnəti]
    = a linguistic community *eine Sprach-
    gemeinschaft*
a phrase book *ein Sprachführer*
a good command of English
    gute englische Sprachkenntnisse

CHECKPOINT ⟨ *In English, please!*

a *zur Entwicklung unabhängiger Sprachvarianten des Englischen führen*
b *die Kommunikation zwischen Menschen*
c *eine gemeinsame Sprache haben/sprechen*

13 **the spread of English** [spred]	*die Verbreitung/Ausbreitung des Englischen*	v **spread, spread, spread** *(sich) ausbreiten*
colonialism [kə'ləʊnɪəlɪzəm]	*Kolonialismus*	N **colony** ['kɒləni] *Kolonie* A **colonial** [kə'ləʊnɪəl] *Kolonial..., kolonial*
15 **varieties of English** [və'raɪətiz]	*verschiedene Arten des Englischen; Varietäten des Englischen*	**variety** 1. *Art, Sorte;* 2. *Vielfalt;* 3. *Abwechslung* v **vary** ['veəri ☆ 'veri] *variieren, unterschiedlich sein* A **various** ['veərɪəs] *verschiedene, mehrere*
English-based pidgin ['pɪdʒɪn]	*Pidginenglisch (= vereinfachte Mischsprache aus Englisch und einer anderen Sprache)*	= **pidgin English** ! homophones: **pidgin – pigeon** ['pɪdʒɪn] *Taube*
English-based creole ['kriːəʊl]	*auf dem Englischen basierendes Kreol[isch] (= als Muttersprache gesprochene Mischsprache aus Englisch und einer nicht europäischen Sprache)*	= **English creole**
17 **a contact language** ['kɒntækt]	*eine Kontaktsprache, eine Mischsprache*	! stress: **contact** ['--] v **contact** *sich in Verbindung setzen mit, kontaktieren*
20 **mother tongue** [,mʌðə 'tʌŋ]	*Muttersprache*	= **native language** ◊ **foreign language** *Fremdsprache* ! pronunciation: **tongue** [tʌŋ]
22 **ethnic identification** [,eθnɪk_aɪ,dentɪfɪ'keɪʃn]	*ethnische Zugehörigkeit*	v **identify** [aɪ'dentɪfaɪ] *identifizieren*
24 **Black English**	*das Englisch der schwarzen US-Bevölkerung, afroamerikanisches Englisch*	= **African American English**

3   An English invasion?

25 The association English has with British colonialism and American hegemony sometimes evokes antagonism towards the English language. In fact, its increasing worldwide influence is seen as an expression of linguistic imperialism, especially because:

30 • English is still one of the official languages in most of the countries of the former Empire.
• English is the dominant language in most international organizations, thus reducing the status of other languages.
• English has endangered the existence of other languages,
35   many of which have become extinct. By doing so, it has reduced the world's linguistic and cultural diversity.
• Promoting the teaching and learning of English is often seen as a neo-colonial form of expanding Western ideas, life-styles and products via language. This holds especially true
40   for the developments of mass entertainment (Hollywood, television), communication technology (the Internet) and consumer goods (fast food).
• The excessive influence of English on established languages, above all through lexical invasion, also gives cause for concern.

Collocations with 'language'

official language [ə'fɪʃl] *Amtssprache*
dominant language ['dɒmɪnənt] *domi-nante Sprache, vorherrschende Sprache*
first/second language *Erst-/Zweitsprache*
native language *Muttersprache*
foreign language *Fremdsprache*
target language *Zielsprache*
original language *Originalsprache (z.B. eines synchronisierten Filmes)*
national language *Nationalsprache, Landessprache*
international language *internationale Sprache*
global/world/universal language *Weltsprache*
technical language *Fachsprache*
colloquial language *Umgangssprache*
❗ **bad language** *(no pl) beleidigende Sprache, unanständige Ausdrücke*

CHECKPOINT — *In English, please!*

a *eine Abneigung gegenüber der englischen Sprache hervorrufen*
b *das Englischlernen fördern*
c *westlich geprägte Vorstellungen mittels Sprache verbreiten*

26 **hegemony** [hɪˈgemǝni, hɪˈdʒemǝni, ˈhedʒɪmǝni] (fml)	*Hegemonie, staatliche Vorherrschaft*	❗ stress: **hegemony** [-ˈ---] or <u>**hegemony**</u> [ˈ----] **political and military hegemony**
antagonism towards the English language [ænˈtægǝnɪzǝm]	*Feindseligkeit gegenüber der englischen Sprache*	= **hostility** [hɒˈstɪlǝti] **towards English** ❗ stress: **antagonism** [-ˈ----] A **antagonistic** [æn,tægǝˈnɪstɪk] *feindlich*
28 **linguistic imperialism** [lɪŋˌgwɪstɪk‿ɪmˈpɪǝriǝlɪzm]	*linguistischer Imperialismus, Sprachimperialismus*	= **language imperialism** N **linguistics** [lɪŋˈgwɪstɪks] *Sprachwissenschaft* N **linguist** [ˈlɪŋgwɪst] *Sprachwissenschaftler/in* A **imperial** [ɪmˈpɪǝriǝl] *kaiserlich, Kaiser...*
34 **endanger** sb./sth. [ɪnˈdeɪndʒǝ]	*jdn./etw. gefährden*	**be/pose a danger to** sb./sth. *eine Gefahr für jdn./etw. sein/darstellen* A **dangerous** *gefährlich*
35 **become extinct** [ɪkˈstɪŋkt]	*aussterben*	= **die out** A **extinct** *ausgestorben* N **extinction** [ɪkˈstɪŋkʃn] *Aussterben, Untergang*
36 **linguistic and cultural diversity** [daɪˈvɜːsǝti]	*sprachliche und kulturelle Vielfalt*	= **linguistic and cultural variety** A **diverse** [daɪˈvɜːs] *verschieden, unterschiedlich*
41 **communication technology** [tekˈnɒlǝdʒi]	*Kommunikationstechnologie, Kommunikationstechnik*	V **communicate** [kǝˈmjuːnɪkeɪt] *kommunizieren* A **communicative** [kǝˈmjuːnɪkǝtɪv ☆ -keɪtɪv] *mitteilsam, gesprächig, kommunikativ* ❗ pronunciation: **technology** [teˈkˈnɒlǝdʒi] *Technik (= Fertigkeit, Methode, Arbeitstechnik)* = **technique** [tekˈniːk]
44 **lexical invasion** [ɪnˈveɪʒn]	*lexikalische Invasion; das Eindringen fremdsprachiger Begriffe in die Muttersprache*	**lexical items** = **words and phrases** V **invade** [ɪnˈveɪd] *einmarschieren in, einfallen in*

4 The future of the English language

45 Some modern linguists are worried that the rise of a great number of 'Englishes' might hamper communication between English-speaking people around the world and, as a consequence, the role of English as an international lingua franca. They also fear that English used and learned 50 universally will be reduced to an elementary skill, a business tool, and may lose its qualities as a language of culture.

However, most politicians and educators agree that there should not be any protective measures taken either to control or to promote the spread of English. There seems to be only one 55 reasonable way to save English as a global language and to keep as many languages alive in the world language system: by encouraging people to learn as many languages as possible to a high level of proficiency.

BACALL

'Yes, I am bilingual. I speak English and Computerese.'

CHECKPOINT — *In English, please!*

a *die Rolle des Englischen als internationale Verkehrssprache beeinträchtigen*
b *Englisch überall verwenden und lernen*
c *die Verbreitung des Englischen begrenzen oder befördern*
d *möglichst viele Sprachen lernen*

'control' – 'check'

control sth. **1.** *etw. beherrschen, die Kontrolle über etw. ausüben;* **2.** *etw. regeln, etw. steuern, etw. bestimmen*
check sth. *etw. überprüfen, etw. kontrollieren*
check up on sb. *jdn. kontrollieren; kontrollieren, was jd. tut*

46 **hamper communication** ['hæmpə]	*die Kommunikation behindern*	◆ improve communication
49 **lingua franca** (usu. sing) [ˌlɪŋgwə 'fræŋkə]	*Lingua franca, Verkehrssprache*	= a shared language used for communication purposes when the speakers have different first languages
52 **educator** (fml) ['edʒukeɪtə]	*Pädagoge, Pädagogin*	v **educate** ['edʒukeɪt] *ausbilden, unterrichten* N **education** [ˌedʒu'keɪʃn] *Ausbildung, Bildung*
53 **protective measure** [prəˌtektɪv 'meʒə]	*Schutzmaßnahme*	v **protect** [prə'tekt] *(be)schützen* N **protection** [prə'tekʃn] *Schutz* **!** pronunciation: **measure** ['meʒə] **take measures** *Maßnahmen ergreifen/treffen*
54 **promote** sth. [prə'məʊt]	*etw. fördern*	**promote** sb. *jdn. befördern* N **promotion** [prə'məʊʃn] **1.** *Förderung (einer guten Sache)*; *Werbeaktion*; **2.** *Beförderung, Aufstieg* **!** *Promotion (zum Doktor)* = **doctorate** ['dɒktərət], **PhD** [ˌpiː_eɪtʃ 'diː]
56 **the world language system**	*das globale Sprachsystem*	**!** stress: **system** ['--] A **systematic** [ˌsɪstə'mætɪk] *systematisch*
58 **a high level of proficiency** [prə'fɪʃnsi]	*ein hoher Kompetenzgrad, ein hohes Leistungsniveau*	**proficiency in/at** (doing) sth. A **proficient** [prə'fɪʃnt] *fähig, gut (im Beruf, in einer Sprache usw.)* **be proficient in English** *die englische Sprache beherrschen*

adapt attention playscript gesture dialogue
Bard performance expression revenge
fate play threat predetermined master age stage dogma replica
comedy foreign monologue playwright golden age costume struggle
timeless history power theme achievement
world play arts scenery
view Elizabethan traditional tragedy playhouse
lines theatre Age props profit
stage company character show
direction draw spectators entertainment antiquated upheaval actor
transcript works of groundlings
drama role Shakespeare
produce crowd

Shakespeare

1 Shakespeare's plays

Four hundred years after his death, William Shakespeare (1564–1616) is still rated as the foremost playwright of the modern world. He wrote about three dozen plays – mainly comedies and tragedies, but also history plays which tell the story of his nation before the reign of his monarch, Elizabeth I.

GET THE CONTEXT

■ **Shakespeare's plays**

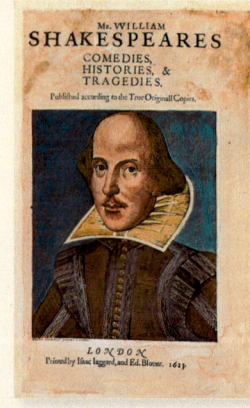

Comedies
- All's Well That Ends Well
- As You Like It
- The Comedy of Errors
- Cymbeline
- Love's Labours Lost
- Measure for Measure
- The Merry Wives of Windsor
- The Merchant of Venice
- A Midsummer Night's Dream
- Much Ado About Nothing
- Pericles, Prince of Tyre
- The Taming of the Shrew
- The Tempest
- Troilus and Cressida
- Twelfth Night
- Two Gentlemen of Verona
- The Winter's Tale

Tragedies
- Antony and Cleopatra
- Coriolanus
- Hamlet
- Julius Caesar
- King Lear
- Macbeth
- Othello
- Romeo and Juliet
- Timon of Athens
- Titus Andronicus

History plays
- Henry IV, Part I
- Henry IV, Part II
- Henry VI, Part I
- Henry VI, Part II
- Henry VI, Part III
- Henry VIII
- King John
- Richard II
- Richard III

2 **be rated (as)** sth.	*als etw. gelten*	**be highly rated** *hoch angesehen sein* **rate** sb./sth. **as ...** *jdn./etw. halten für ...* N **rating** *Bewertung, Einschätzung; Stellenwert*
playwright ['pleɪraɪt]	*Bühnenschriftsteller/in, Stückeschreiber/in*	= **dramatist** ['dræmətɪst] *Dramatiker/in* ! Not: ~~playwriter~~ Remember: **writer** *Schriftsteller/in*
3 **play**	*Theaterstück, Schauspiel*	V **play** *spielen (auch eine Rolle im Theater)* ! *ein Spiel spielen/machen* = **play a game**
4 **comedy** ['kɒmədi]	*Komödie, Lustspiel*	! stress: **comedy** ['---] A **comic** ['kɒmɪk] *komisch, witzig* N **comedian** [kə'miːdiən] *Komiker/in*
tragedy ['trædʒədi]	*Tragödie, Trauerspiel*	! stress: **tragedy** ['---] A **tragic** ['trædʒɪk] *tragisch*
history play	*Historiendrama, Historienspiel*	A **historical** [hɪ'stɒrɪkl] *geschichtlich, historisch*

2 A voice of his time

The Elizabethan Age is often remembered as a golden age for its many achievements in the arts. However, England was struggling for peace and stability at home and against threats from foreign powers abroad. Religious, social, political and
10 economic developments challenged society.

People were torn between a traditional world view and a more modern one; they generally accepted the Earth as the centre of the cosmos and the Church as the centre of life on Earth, but were keen to discover new truths beyond the old dogmas. Was
15 Man master of his own fate or was his fate predetermined? What would happen if people left their place in society? Every year, men set out to discover new lands overseas, trading and making huge profits – all around, things were on the move. Shakespeare's drama reflects this upheaval.

Elizabeth I, Queen of England from 1558 until her death in 1603

'man' = German 'der Mensch'

Man has traditionally been used to mean 'all men and women':
   early/modern/prehistoric man
Most people now prefer one of these terms:
   humanity [hjuːˈmænəti] *die Menschheit*
   human beings *die Menschen*
   people *die Leute, die Menschen*

CHECKPOINT *In English, please!*

a hin und her gerissen sein zwischen einer traditionellen und einer modernen Weltsicht

b darauf aus sein, neue Wahrheiten zu entdecken

c sich aufmachen, um neue Länder in Übersee zu entdecken

d riesige Gewinne machen

6 **the Elizabethan Age** [ɪˌlɪzəˈbiːθən]	*das Elisabethanische Zeitalter (= die Regierungszeit von Elisabeth I. von 1558–1603)*	**!** **Elizabethan** [ɪˌlɪzəˈbiːθn] – **Elizabeth** [ɪˈlɪzəbəθ] **age** **1.** *Lebensalter;* **2.** *Zeitalter*
golden age	*Goldenes Zeitalter; Blütezeit*	**!** *ein goldener Ring, ein Ring aus Gold =* **a gold ring**
7 **achievements in the arts** [əˈtʃiːvmənts]	*künstlerische Errungenschaften*	v **achieve** *erreichen, schaffen* **the arts** (pl) *(die) Kunst, die Künste, (die) Kultur*
8 **struggle for sth.** [ˈstrʌgl]	*um etw. ringen*	**struggle for breath** *nach Luft ringen* N **struggle** *Kampf*
threats from foreign powers [θrets, ˈfɒrən]	*von fremden/ausländischen Mächten ausgehende (Be-)Drohungen*	v **threaten** [ˈθretn] *(be)drohen* N **foreigner** [ˈfɒrənə] *Fremde(r), Ausländer/in* A **powerful** *mächtig*
11 **a traditional world view** [vjuː]	*eine traditionelle Weltan-schauung*	N **tradition** [trəˈdɪʃn] *Tradition* v **view** *betrachten*
14 **the old dogmas** [ˈdɒgməz] (often disapproving)	*die alten Dogmen, die alten un-umstößlichen Lehrmeinungen*	A **dogmatic** [dɒgˈmætɪk] *dogmatisch*
15 **be master of one's own fate** [ˈmɑːstə]	*sein Schicksal selbst in die Hand nehmen*	**be master of the situation** *Herr der Lage sein* **be one's own master** *sein eigener Herr sein*
predetermined [ˌpriːdɪˈtɜːmɪnd]	*vorherbestimmt*	v **predetermine** (fml) *vorherbestimmen*
18 **profit** [ˈprɒfɪt]	*Gewinn, Profit*	**!** stress: **pro**fit [ˈ--] v **profit** *profitieren* A **profitable** [ˈprɒfɪtəbl] *gewinnbringend, nützlich*
19 **drama** [ˈdrɑːmə]	*Drama, Schauspiel; Dramatik*	A **dramatic** [drəˈmætɪk] *dramatisch* N **dramatist** [ˈdræmətɪst] *Dramatiker/in*
upheaval [ʌpˈhiːvl]	*Umbruch, Umwälzung, Aufruhr*	= **disruption** [dɪsˈrʌpʃn]

3 The age of theatre

20 Shakespeare was a businessman, too, who invested in the theatre companies that produced his plays. Much more than today, theatre was a popular form of entertainment which could draw over 2500 spectators to a show, from aristocrats to apprentices.

25 The playhouses were open to the sky and the platform stage had almost no scenery. It was surrounded on three sides by the groundlings (those standing on the ground) who took a lively part in the performance. So the actors (only men, as women were not allowed to perform on stage) had to use
30 all their skills of speech, expression and gesture to hold the crowd's attention. Spectacular costumes and realistic props helped.

A view of the Globe Theatre from among the groundlings

German 'Zuschauer', 'Publikum'

spectators [spekˈteɪtəz ☆ ˈspekteɪtərz] / crowd [kraʊd] (vor allem bei einem Sportereignis oder einer sonstigen Veranstaltung)
audience [ˈɔːdiəns] (im Kino, Theater, Konzert, bei einem Vortrag usw.)
viewers (= TV audience) (beim Fernsehen)

21	**theatre company** [ˌθɪətə ˈkʌmpəni]	Theatergesellschaft, Theaterkompanie, Ensemble	**theatre** (BE) = **theater** (AE)
	produce a play [prəˈdjuːs]	ein Theaterstück inszenieren/einstudieren/aufführen	N **production** [prəˈdʌkʃn] (Theater-)Inszenierung, (Film-)Produktion, Regie N **producer** Regisseur/in, (Film-)Produzent/in
22	**entertainment** [ˌentəˈteɪnmənt]	Unterhaltung	V **entertain** sb. jdn. unterhalten, amüsieren
23	**draw sb.** [drɔː], **drew, drawn**	(Zuschauer, Besucher usw.) anziehen, anlocken	= **attract** sb.
	show	(Theater-)Vorstellung; Show	**go to / see / watch a show** ins Theater gehen
25	**playhouse** [ˈpleɪhaʊs]	Schauspielhaus, Theater	= **theatre**
	stage [steɪdʒ]	Bühne	V **stage** aufführen, veranstalten
26	**scenery** [ˈsiːnəri]	Bühnenbild, Kulisse	N **scene** [siːn] Szene
27	**the groundlings** [ˈɡraʊndlɪŋz]	das Stehplatzpublikum, die Leute auf den billigen Plätzen	
28	**performance** [pəˈfɔːməns]	Aufführung, Vorführung	V **perform** aufführen; auftreten
	actor [ˈæktə]	Schauspieler/in	V **act** (Part, Rolle) spielen
30	**expression** [ɪkˈspreʃn]	Ausdruck, Ausdruckskraft	V **express** [ɪkˈspres] ausdrücken, äußern
	gesture [ˈdʒestʃə]	Gestik, Geste	! pronunciation: **gesture** [ˈdʒestʃə] V **gesture** eine Handbewegung machen
	hold the crowd's attention [kraʊd, əˈtenʃn], **held, held**	die Aufmerksamkeit des Publikums aufrechterhalten	= **keep the spectators' attention**
31	**costume** [ˈkɒstjuːm]	Kostüm	! stress: **costume** [ˈ--]
	props (usu. pl)	Requisiten	= **stage props**

4 Playscripts

To make it difficult for rivals to steal the plays, actors were not given complete playscripts to learn their lines
35 from, but used a transcript showing only their own role. Modern playscripts, of course, show the spoken text, i.e. the dialogue and monologues, for all the characters. There are few stage directions in Shakespeare's plays, and we are not sure if Shakespeare actually wrote them.

'Page 33, line 4 …'

34 **learn** one's **lines**	*seinen (Rollen-)Text lernen, seine Rolle lernen*	**a line from the film 'Shakespeare in Love'** *ein Satz aus dem Film „Shakespeare in Love"*
35 **transcript** ['trænskrıpt]	*Abschrift, Kopie*	also: **transcription** [træn'skrıpʃn]
role	*Rolle; Part*	= **part** **get/have/play the leading role** *... die Hauptrolle* ❗ homophones: **role – roll** *Rolle (aus Papier usw.)*
37 **dialogue** (AE also **dialog**) ['daıəlɒg]	*Dialog*	❗ stress: **dialogue** ['---]
monologue (AE also **monolog**) ['mɒnəlɒg]	*Monolog*	❗ stress: **monologue** ['---] = **soliloquy** [sə'lıləkwi] *Monolog allein auf der Bühne*
character ['kærəktə]	*Charakter, Figur* (in Buch, Film usw.)	❗ stress: **character** ['---] **the main character** *die Hauptfigur, die Hauptperson* N **characteristic** [ˌkærəktə'rıstık] *(charakteristisches) Merkmal* N **characterization** [ˌkærəktəraı'zeıʃn] *Charakterisierung*

■ Reading drama

A play cannot be read in the same way as a novel or short story. Why is that?

- Plays are written mainly to be performed, not to be read.
- Most plays are written from the points of view of various **characters**. (Plays for one character are rather rare.)
- Plays consist of a series of speeches and **stage directions**. When reading a play, you try to imagine it on stage, with the characters' expressions, gestures, movements, actions, tone of voice, etc.

- **Dramatic dialogue** may sound like real-life dialogue but it's very different. It cuts out unnecessary talking and is used to reveal more about a character and their motives, to give crucial information, build suspense, highlight important moments, create a dramatic climax or move the action forward.

5 The Bard today

40 The works that 'the Bard' left behind have been translated into nearly every language and adapted for every kind of media, from comics and musicals to paintings and films. Millions of tourists visit the town of his birth and death, Stratford-upon-Avon, and the replica of his playhouse, the London Globe.

45 Shakespeare's language may seem antiquated at first, but when his plays are performed – or just read aloud – his words come alive. Shakespeare's themes – ambition, revenge, love – are timeless.

'Romeo and Juliet met online in a chat room. But their relationship ended tragically when Juliet's computer crashed.'

GET THE CONTEXT

■ **Quotes from Shakespeare's plays** *Zitate aus Shakespeare-Stücken*

I will wear my heart upon my sleeve. (from: **Othello**)
Ich werde mein/das Herz auf der Zunge tragen.
(wear your heart on your sleeve = show your true feelings openly)

Something is rotten in the state of Denmark. (from: **Hamlet**)
Etwas ist faul im Staate Dänemark.

All that glisters is not gold. (from: **The Merchant of Venice**)
Es ist nicht alles Gold, was glänzt.
(modern saying: All that glitters/glistens is not gold.)

All's well that ends well. (from: **All's Well That Ends Well**)
Ende gut, alles gut.

It smells to heaven. (from: **Hamlet**)
Es stinkt zum Himmel.

too much of a good thing (from: **As You Like It**)
zu viel des Guten

It's all Greek to me. (from: **Julius Caesar**)
Es ist mir ganz unverständlich. / Ich verstehe nur Bahnhof.

Love is blind. (from: **The Merchant of Venice**)
Liebe macht blind.

40 **work**	*Werk* (Buch, Gemälde usw.)	**a work of art** *ein Kunstwerk* **the collected/complete works of Shakespeare** *Shakespeares gesammelte/sämtliche Werke*
the Bard [bɑːd]	*der Barde, der Dichter* (häufige Bezeichnung für Shakespeare)	= **the Bard of Avon** ['eɪvn] **bard** (literary) = **a person who writes poems**
41 **adapt** sth. **(for** sth.**)** [ə'dæpt]	*etw. (für etw.) bearbeiten*	**adapt a novel for television** *einen Roman (zum* *Verfilmen) fürs Fernsehen bearbeiten* N **adaptation** [ˌædæp'teɪʃn] *Bearbeitung (eines* *Romans, Theaterstücks usw.)* ❗ **ad**o**pt** [ə'dɒpt] *adoptieren; übernehmen*
44 **replica** ['replɪkə]	*Nachbau; Reproduktion, Kopie*	= **a very good or exact copy of something**
45 **antiquated** ['æntɪkweɪtɪd]	*veraltet, überholt* (Dinge oder Ansichten)	= **outdated, old-fashioned** (and no longer suitable for modern conditions) A|N **antique** [æn'tiːk] **1.** *antik (= alt und wertvoll –* *vor allem mit Bezug auf Möbel, Schmuck usw.);* **2.** *Antiquität*
47 **theme** [θiːm]	*(immer wiederkehrendes)* *Thema; Leitmotiv*	**introduce a theme** *in ein Thema einführen* **develop a theme** *ein Thema entwickeln/entfalten* ❗ *Thema (= Gesprächsthema, Sachgebiet)* = **subject** ['sʌbdʒɪkt]
revenge [rɪ'vendʒ]	*Rache*	**take** (one's) **revenge on** sb. *sich an jdm. rächen*
48 **timeless** ['taɪmləs] (fml)	*zeitlos* (Schönheit usw.)	N **timelessness** *Zeitlosigkeit, Unvergänglichkeit*

VOCAB for Text Analysis

abridged [ə'brɪdʒd]	*gekürzt*	An **abridged** version of a text is a shortened version.
act	*Akt*	Traditionally, plays are divided into **acts**.
action ['ækʃn]	*Handlung*	= everything that happens in a story or play **External action** describes actual events that happen. **Internal action** is what goes on in a character's mind.
acrostic [ə'krɒstɪk]	*Akrostichon*	= a poem in which the first letters of the lines form a word or phrase
adapted	*bearbeitet, adaptiert*	An **adapted** text has been changed to be suitable for its readers.
alliteration [ə,lɪtə'reɪʃn]	*Alliteration*	= repetition of the same consonant sound in words close together in a poem, e.g. 'Along came a crowd of crazy cats.'
antonym ['æntənɪm]	*Antonym, Gegenwort*	'Slow' is an **antonym** of 'fast'.
article ['ɑːtɪkl]	*Artikel*	= a story report in a newspaper or magazine **print article** *gedruckter Artikel* **online article** *Artikel im Internet*
assonance ['æsənəns]	*Assonanz*	= repetition of the same vowel sound in words close together, e.g. [əʊ] in 'Oh no, my mobile's broken.'
atmosphere ['ætməsfɪə]	*Atmosphäre, Stimmung*	= the feeling or mood created in a piece of literature
audiobook ['ɔːdiəʊbʊk]	*Hörbuch*	= a sound recording of a book
author ['ɔːθə]	*Schriftsteller/in, Autor/in*	= the writer of a piece of literature

biography [baɪˈɒɡrəfi] *Biografie*	= the story of a person's life **autobiography** [ˌɔːtəʊbaɪˈɒɡrəfi] = the story of a person's life written by that person
character [ˈkærəktə] *Figur, Charakter*	= a person in a story; the qualities of a person **main character** *Hauptfigur*
characterization [ˌkærəktəraɪˈzeɪʃn] *Figurencharakterisierung*	= the way an author presents characters to readers **Implicit** or **indirect characterization** is when the reader finds out about a character through his/her words, actions. **Explicit** or **direct characterization** is when the author describes a person's character.
chorus [ˈkɔːrəs] *Refrain*	= a part of a song that is sung after each verse
chronological [ˌkrɒnəˈlɒdʒɪkl] *chronologisch*	= (events) arranged as they happened in time
climax [ˈklaɪmæks] *Höhepunkt*	= the most exciting or important point in the action of a story or play
collection *Sammlung, Anthologie*	= a number of short stories or poems in one book
comedy [ˈkɒmədi] *Komödie, Lustspiel*	= a play, often meant to be funny or amusing, with a happy ending
conflict [ˈkɒnflɪkt] *Konflikt, Widerstreit*	= the key struggle between different characters in a piece of literature
context [ˈkɒntekst] *Zusammenhang, Kontext*	= the situation in which events happen and which helps you understand them
dialogue (AE also **dialog**) [ˈdaɪəlɒɡ] *Dialog*	= conversation in a story or play between two or more people
drama [ˈdrɑːmə] *Drama, Theater, Schauspiel, Stück*	If you like acting, join the school **drama** club. A **dramatic** [drəˈmætɪk] *dramatisch*

dystopia [dɪs'təʊpɪə]	*Dystopie*	= an imaginary place or society in which life is terrible or a piece of literature describing such a place
ending	*Schluss, Ende*	Most comedies have happy **endings**.
essay ['eseɪ]	*Aufsatz, Essay*	= a short piece of writing on a particular subject, often written at school or university
event	*Ereignis*	The **events** of a story make up the plot.
exaggeration [ɪg,zædʒə'reɪʃn]	*Übertreibung*	**Exaggeration** makes characters or events larger than life and memorable.
extract ['ekstrækt]	*Auszug*	= a part taken from a longer piece of literature
fairy tale	*Märchen*	= a traditional fantasy story
fantasy ['fæntəsi]	*Fantasie*	= a story set in an imagined world where unreal or unlikely things happen
fiction ['fɪkʃn]	*Erzählliteratur, Belletristik*	*Robinson Crusoe* is a famous work of **fiction**.
flashback ['flæʃbæk]	*Rückblende*	Events that happened before the story takes place are sometimes told in **flashbacks**.
foreshadowing [fɔː'ʃædəʊɪŋ]	*Vorahnung, Andeutung*	What she saw in her dream was a **foreshadowing** of what would happen the next day.
genre ['ʒɒ̃rə, 'ʒɒnrə]	*Genre, Gattung*	= a type or style of literature, e.g. science fiction
heading	*Überschrift*	= a title printed at the beginning of a text
headline	*Schlagzeile, Überschrift*	= the heading of a newspaper article, especially on the front page
hero, heroine ['hɪərəʊ, 'herəʊɪn]	*Held, Heldin*	= the main character in a piece of literature
humour (BE) **/ humor** (AE) ['hjuːmə]	*Humor; humoristischer Text*	= what makes something funny; a piece of funny writing

image ['ɪmɪdʒ]	*Bild, Vorstellung*	The **images** the writer uses help you to create pictures in your mind.
imagery ['ɪmɪdʒəri]	*bildhafte Sprache, Metaphorik*	Metaphors and similes are both types of **imagery**.
irony ['aɪrəni]	*Ironie*	= humorous use of words saying the opposite of what you really mean A **ironic** [aɪ'rɒnɪk] *ironisch*
line	*Zeile*	A sonnet always has 14 **lines**.
lyrics ['lɪrɪks]	*Text eines Lieds*	I don't like the music but the **lyrics** are great.
message	*Botschaft, Aussage*	The **message** of the story is: love is wonderful but it can also hurt.
metaphor ['metəfə]	*Metapher*	'He looked at us with *eyes of stone*' – that's a very strong **metaphor**. A **metaphorical** [ˌmetə'fɒrɪkl] *metaphorisch*
metre (BE) **/ meter** (AE) ['miːtə]	*Metrum*	= a regular rhythm pattern in a poem
monologue (AE also **monolog**) ['mɒnəlɒg]	*Monolog*	= a long speech in a play by one person, especially when alone
moral ['mɒrəl]	*Moral*	= the message of a piece of literature or something that you can learn from it
motif [məʊ'tiːf]	*Motiv, Leitgedanke*	= a subject, idea or phrase that is developed in the course of a piece of literature
narrator [nə'reɪtə ☆ 'næreɪtər]	*Erzähler*	= the character or 'voice' in a piece of literature who is telling the story, not the same as the author **first-person narrator** *Ich-Erzähler* **third-person narrator** *personaler Erzähler* **omniscient narrator** [ɒm'nɪsiənt] *allwissender, auktorialer Erzähler*

non-fiction	*nicht fiktionale Texte, Sachtexte*	I never read novels. I prefer **non-fiction**.
novel ['nɒvl]	*Roman*	= a long and complex fictional piece of narrative prose often divided into chapters
novelist ['nɒvəlɪst]	*Romanautor/in*	My favourite **novelist** is James Joyce.
open-ended	*offen, nicht entschieden*	In an **open-ended** story, the reader is left to think about what really happens.
parody ['pærədi]	*Parodie*	= a piece of writing that copies the style of something or somebody to be amusing
perform [pə'fɔːm]	*auftreten; aufführen*	The actor Jon Wyatt **performed** as Hamlet last night. Our drama club is **performing** *Woyzeck* next month.
performance [pə'fɔːməns]	*Vorstellung, Auftritt*	Wyatt's **performance** was described as 'fantastic'.
personification [pə,sɒnɪfɪ'keɪʃn]	*Verkörperung, Personifizierung*	= representing something (an object, an animal, an idea) as a person
perspective [pə'spektɪv]	*Blickwinkel, Perspektive*	= the point of view from which a character sees things
play	*Stück, Schauspiel*	*Hamlet* is probably the most famous **play** in English literature.
playwright ['pleɪraɪt]	*Dramatiker/in*	= someone who writes plays
plot	*Handlung, Plot*	= the sequence of events of a story or play
poem	*Gedicht*	I prefer **poems** to novels because of their rhythm and imagery.
poet	*Dichter/in*	= someone who writes poems
poetry	*Lyrik*	I love literature but almost never read **poetry**.

point of view	*Standpunkt, Erzähl-perspektive*	= the situation from which a character sees, writes or evaluates something **unlimited/limited point of view** *unbegrenzte/begrenzte Perspektive*
production [prə'dʌkʃn]	*Inszenierung, Aufführung*	There is a great new **production** of *The Mousetrap* at our local theatre.
prose	*Prosa*	= writing that is not poetry or drama
protagonist [prə'tægənɪst]	*Protagonist/in*	= a main character in a piece of literature
punchline ['pʌntʃlaɪn]	*Pointe*	= the last (often surprising) sentence or few words of a joke or story that make it funny
quotation [kwəʊ'teɪʃn]	*Zitat*	= a short extract from a piece of literature that shows something interesting or useful
realistic [ˌriːə'lɪstɪk]	*realistisch*	A **realistic** story shows things as they really are.
recite [rɪ'saɪt]	*vortragen, rezitieren*	Learn the poem so you can **recite** it to the class.
register ['redʒɪstə]	*Register, Stilebene*	= the level and style of a text
repetition [ˌrepə'tɪʃn]	*Wiederholung*	Songs and poetry often create effects by use of **repetition**.
resolution [ˌrezə'luːʃn]	*Auflösung, Lösung*	= the moment at the end of a drama, novel, etc., where all the conflicts are solved
review [rɪ'vjuː]	*Besprechung, Rezension*	= a report discussing a piece of literature or a film and giving an opinion on it
rhyme [raɪm]	**1.** *Reim;* **2.** *sich reimen*	= a word that has or ends in the same sound as another word, e.g. *cat* **rhymes** with *hat* **end-rhyme** *Endreim* **internal rhyme** *Reim inmitten der Zeile* **rhyme scheme** [skiːm] *Reimschema*

rhythm ['rɪðəm]	*Rhythmus*	= the pattern of stress in a poem
satire ['sætaɪə]	*Satire*	= a piece of writing criticizing someone or something by making fun of them so that people will clearly see their faults
scene [siːn]	*Szene*	A play or the acts of a play are divided into **scenes**.
science fiction (SF)	*Science-Fiction*	= a genre that deals with imagined results of scientific discoveries, usually in the future
setting	*Schauplatz, Handlungsrahmen*	= the time and place and sometimes the atmosphere of a piece of literature
be set in	*spielen in*	The novel **is set in** Alabama in the 1950s.
simile ['sɪməliː]	*Vergleich*	= a poetic device comparing one thing to another, e.g. 'Her skin was white as snow'
sonnet ['sɒnɪt ☆ 'sɑːnɪt]	*Sonett*	= a poem with a fixed rhyme pattern and 14 lines of 10 or 11 syllables each
speech	*Rede, Sprechbeitrag*	I only had a small part in the play, just three **speeches**.
stage directions ['steɪdʒ dəˌrekʃnz]	*Bühnen-, Regieanweisungen*	= notes in a play describing the scene and telling actors when to enter and exit and what to do
stanza ['stænzə]	*Strophe*	Poems are often divided into **stanzas** or verses.
stereotype ['sterɪətaɪp]	*Klischeevorstellung, Stereotyp*	I can't identify with this character. She's just the **stereotype** of a romantic schoolgirl.
story	*Geschichte, Erzählung*	*Treasure Island* is an exciting **story**.
short story [ˌ-'--]	*Kurzgeschichte*	'The Garden Party' is a famous **short story** by Katherine Mansfield.
stress	1. *Betonung;* 2. *betonen*	Each line of a sonnet has five **stressed** syllables.
style [staɪl]	*Stil*	= the particular way in which a piece of literature is written

stylistic device [staɪˌlɪstɪk dɪˈvaɪs]	*Stilmittel, Stilfigur*	Poets create effects with **stylistic devices** like metaphors, rhymes or repetition.
suspense [səˈspens]	*Spannung*	It's a great thriller, full of **suspense**.
symbol [ˈsɪmbl]	*Symbol*	A heart is a **symbol** of love. A **symbolic** [sɪmˈbɒlɪk] *symbolisch*
synonym [ˈsɪnənɪm]	*Synonym (= Wort mit identischer oder ähnlicher Bedeutung)*	= a word that means the same as another word, like *big = large*
tension [ˈtenʃn]	*Spannung*	The atmosphere of **tension** in the book makes it so exciting.
text	*Text*	= any form of written material **argumentative text** [ˌɑːɡjuˈmentətɪv] *Erörterung* **descriptive text** *Beschreibung* **expository text** [ɪkˈspɒzətri] *Darlegung* **fictional text** *Erzähltext* **instructive text** *Lehrtext* **non-fictional text** *Sachtext*
text type [taɪp]	*Textsorte*	An argumentative text is a common **text type** in exams.
title [ˈtaɪtl]	*Titel*	= the name of a piece of literature
tone [təʊn]	*Ton*	Roald Dahl's poems always have a humorous **tone**.
tragedy [ˈtrædʒədi]	*Tragödie*	= a serious play with an unhappy ending, in which the main character(s) often die(s)
utopia [juːˈtəʊpɪə]	*Utopie*	= a story about an imagined place where everything is perfect
verse [vɜːs]	*Vers, Dichtung; Strophe*	A narrative poem is a story told in **verse**.
free verse	*freier Vers, reimlose Dichtung*	= poetry with no regular rhythm or rhyme scheme
writer	*Autor/in, Schriftsteller/in*	= someone who writes

Checkpoints: Suggested Answers

A Being Young

page 14
a Life suddenly becomes complicated.
b sleep in
c stay up late
d concentrate on schoolwork

page 16
a reach sexual maturity
b experience peer pressure
c become sexually active
d have sex without regard for the consequences

page 18
a feel a need to emancipate yourself from your parents
b a time for having fun and experimenting
c talk to your parents about anything openly
d stay clear of dangerous behaviours

page 20
a get grades/marks (BE)
b have clearly defined goals/ambitions
c make decisions about a career
d switch careers at least once in your lifetime

B The Individual in Society

page 24
a be born into a specific social and geographical setting
b social/cultural/religious/political/internal/moral values
c shape an individual's identity
d be conscious/aware of your role (with)in society

page 26
a change over time
b determine an individual's membership of specific groups

c reject mainstream culture
d voluntarily join a political party / join a political party voluntarily

page 28
a feel superior to other members of society
b discriminate against an individual or group
c challenge society's values
d resolve differences (of opinion) through negotiation

C National Identity and Diversity

page 32
a pride in your nation
b identify with the country you were born in
c have at least a vague notion of what the nation stands for
d nothing but a list of stereotypes

page 34
a the belief in a representative democracy
b principles such as equality before the law
c expect new members to obey the laws of their host country
d swear an oath of allegiance to your new country

page 36
a as a result of immigration
b benefit from a mix of cultures
c view the USA as the great 'melting pot'
d distinct parts that make up a successful whole

page 38
a fail to grasp the advantages of diversity
b discriminate against migrants
c force migrants into ethnic ghettos in large cities
d not be in the interest of the migrants

D The United Kingdom

page 42
a be made up of four countries
b develop separately from the rest of Europe
c be a force to be reckoned with
d exert tremendous influence on culture in the western world

page 44
a run the day-to-day affairs of the Church of England / Anglican Church
b consist of a lower house and an upper house
c be elected by the people
d appoint sb. because of (his/her) past service to the nation

page 46
a consist of a body of laws
b undergo huge changes
c exercise powers within the (House of) Lords
d be subject to constitutional reform

page 48
a force schools to compete with one another / each other
b be far from being a classless society
c depend to a large extent on how much money a young person's family has

E The United States of America

page 52
a mean different things to different people
b Anybody can achieve anything.
c consider the USA (to be) 'the greatest country on earth'
d run a country on the principle of personal liberty/freedom

page 56
a draw up a bill of rights / Bill of Rights
b ensure the individual rights of American citizens
c believe in God
d elect sb. President/president

F Regions of the UK and the USA

G Urban, Suburban and Rural Lifestyles

H India

page 84
a disease(s) that left millions of people dead
b grant India independence
c divide the former colony into two separate countries
d maintain huge armies

page 88
a make India an ideal location for call centres
b live and work abroad
c continue to live in extreme poverty
d reap the benefits of the newly found wealth

I Germany in the World

page 92
a mean different things to different people
b produce high-quality goods
c conquer totalitarianism

page 94
a the association of Germany with the Second World War / with World War Two
b the popular press
c the British image of Germany

page 96
a be proud of your heritage
b have (a) limited knowledge of modern Germany
c be interested in broadening your sphere of influence
d be highly critical of America's war in Vietnam

page 98
a be a member of NATO
b keep the peace
c an international conference on the environment
d give Germany a permanent seat on the UN Security Council

J Global Perspectives

page 102
a the elimination of national protectionism
b pass freely from one part of the world to another
c gain access to world markets
d buy goods at lower prices

page 104
a come at the expense of workers
b work long hours
c at home and abroad
d be willing to work for considerably lower wages

page 106
a affect the way workers are treated
b commit yourself to 'ethical manufacturing'
c do your best to avoid bad press
d avoid big brands altogether

M The Media

N The World of English

O Shakespeare

VOCAB Finder